Emma Goldman

These and other titles are included in The Importance
Of biography series:

Alexander the Great	Adolf Hitler
Muhammad Ali	Harry Houdini
Louis Armstrong	Thomas Jefferson
James Baldwin	Mother Jones
Clara Barton	Chief Joseph
Napoleon Bonaparte	Malcolm X
Julius Caesar	Margaret Mead
Rachel Carson	Michelangelo
Charlie Chaplin	Wolfgang Amadeus Mozart
Cesar Chavez	John Muir
Winston Churchill	Sir Isaac Newton
Cleopatra	Richard Nixon
Christopher Columbus	Georgia O'Keeffe
Hernando Cortes	Louis Pasteur
Marie Curie	Pablo Picasso
Amelia Earhart	Elvis Presley
Thomas Edison	Jackie Robinson
Albert Einstein	Norman Rockwell
Duke Ellington	Anwar Sadat
Dian Fossey	Margaret Sanger
Benjamin Franklin	Oskar Schindler
Galileo Galilei	John Steinbeck
Emma Goldman	Jim Thorpe
Jane Goodall	Mark Twain
Martha Graham	Queen Victoria
Stephen Hawking	Pancho Villa
Jim Henson	H. G. Wells

THE IMPORTANCE OF

Emma Goldman

by
Kathlyn Gay and Martin Gay

Lucent Books, P.O. Box 289011, San Diego, CA 92198-9011

Library of Congress Cataloging-in-Publication Data

Gay, Kathlyn.
      The importance of Emma Goldman / by Kathlyn Gay and
      Martin Gay.
          p.   cm.—(The importance of)
      Includes bibliographical references and index.
      Summary: Examines the life and work of the Russian
   immigrant to the United States who attempted to establish
   a social order based on absolute individual liberty.
      ISBN 1-56006-024-7 (lib. bdg. : alk. paper)
      1. Goldman, Emma, 1869–1940—Juvenile literature.
   2. Women anarchists—United States—Biography—Juvenile
   literature.   3. Women political activists—United States—
   Biography—Juvenile literature.   [1. Goldman, Emma, 1869–
   1940.   2. Anarchists.   3. Political activists.   4. Women—
   Biography.]   I. Gay, Martin.   II. Title.   III. Series.
   HX843.7.G65G39   1997
   335'.83'092—dc20   95–2859
   [B]   CIP
                                                                     AC

Copyright 1997 by Lucent Books, Inc., P.O. Box 289011,
San Diego, California, 92198-9011

Printed in the U.S.A.

Contents

Foreword

THE IMPORTANCE OF biography series deals with individuals who have made a unique contribution to history. The editors of the series have deliberately chosen to cast a wide net and include people from all fields of endeavor. Individuals from politics, music, art, literature, philosophy, science, sports, and religion are all represented. In addition, the editors did not restrict the series to individuals whose accomplishments have helped change the course of history. Of necessity, this criterion would have eliminated many whose contribution was great, though limited. Charles Darwin, for example, was responsible for radically altering the scientific view of the natural history of the world. His achievements continue to impact the study of science today. Others, such as Chief Joseph of the Nez Percé, played a pivotal role in the history of their own people. While Joseph's influence does not extend much beyond the Nez Percé, his nonviolent resistance to white expansion and his continuing role in protecting his tribe and his homeland remain an inspiration to all.

These biographies are more than factual chronicles. Each volume attempts to emphasize an individual's contributions both in his or her own time and for posterity. For example, the voyages of Christopher Columbus opened the way to European colonization of the New World. Unquestionably, his encounter with the New World brought monumental changes to both Europe and the Americas in his day. Today, however, the broader impact of Columbus's voyages is being critically scrutinized. *Christopher Columbus,* as well as every biography in The Importance Of series, includes and evaluates the most recent scholarship available on each subject.

Each author includes a wide variety of primary and secondary source quotations to document and substantiate his or her work. All quotes are footnoted to show readers exactly how and where biographers derive their information, as well as provide stepping stones to further research. These quotations enliven the text by giving readers eyewitness views of the life and times of each individual covered in The Importance Of series.

Finally, each volume is enhanced by photographs, bibliographies, chronologies, and comprehensive indexes. For both the casual reader and the student engaged in research, The Importance Of biographies will be a fascinating adventure into the lives of people who have helped shape humanity's past and present, and who will continue to shape its future.

IMPORTANT DATES IN THE LIFE OF EMMA GOLDMAN

1869
Born June 27 in Kovno, Russia.

1876–1877
Moves to Koenigsberg, Germany.

1881–1882
Returns with family to Russia, settling in Saint Petersburg.

1885
Immigrates to the United States.

1886
Settles in Rochester, New York; learns of Haymarket riot in Chicago.

1887
Marries Jacob Kershner, but divorces within the year and moves to New Haven, Connecticut; four Chicago anarchists linked to Haymarket events are executed.

1889
Moves to New York City.

1890
Makes first lecture tour on anarchism.

1892
Carnegie steel plant workers in Homestead, Pennsylvania, strike and battle strikebreakers; Alexander Berkman, Goldman's comrade, attempts assassination of Henry Clay Frick, head of the Carnegie Steel Company; Berkman sentenced to twenty-two years in prison.

1893
Arrested for inciting a riot after speaking at demonstration; sentenced to one-year prison term; learns nursing skills in prison.

1895
Travels to Vienna to study medicine. Further studies in Paris in 1899 are incomplete.

1901
President William McKinley assassinated; Goldman, back in the United States, suspected of conspiracy.

1903
Embarks on extensive lecture tours and organizes Free Speech League.

1906
Cofounds *Mother Earth* magazine; Alexander Berkman released from prison.

1910
Anarchism and Other Essays is published.

1917
United States enters World War I; Goldman founds No-Conscription League to oppose draft; with Berkman, convicted of conspiracy to obstruct the draft and sentenced to two-year prison terms.

1918–1919
Imprisoned at Missouri state prison; Berkman at federal prison in Georgia.

1919
Along with 247 other alien radicals, Goldman and Berkman deported from the United States.

1920–1921
Goldman and Berkman live in Russia, become disillusioned, and leave.

1922–1923
Lives in exile in Sweden and Germany.

1923
My Disillusionment in Russia is published.

1924–1928
Writes and lectures on Russia and social issues, from England and Canada.

1928
Settles in Saint-Tropez, France, and begins writing autobiography.

1931
Living My Life is published.

1934
United States permits Goldman to conduct ninety-day lecture tour.

1936
Berkman commits suicide.

1936–1938
Lectures and raises funds to support Spanish anarchists.

1939
Moves to Canada.

1940
Dies in Toronto.

Outspoken Advocate For Personal Liberty

Emma Goldman, one of the most famous female radicals and activists in the United States during the late 1800s and early 1900s, was primed for activism by firsthand experience. During an impoverished childhood in Russia, Emma and her family witnessed and were victims of the cruelty and oppression of tyrannical rulers, which set the stage for Emma's lifelong fight for economic justice and individual liberty.

Attempting to find a place of peace and comfort away from an abusive home and a repressive government in czarist Russia, Emma immigrated to the United States in December 1885 at the age of sixteen. She was eager to settle into the America of many Europeans' dreams—a free, democratic society. But once there she was stunned by the slavelike working conditions that existed in most factories and appalled by ruthless government suppression of workers' dissent. Soon she began to develop a political philosophy that embraced an anarchist goal: to establish a new social order based on absolute individual liberty unrestricted by government or other authority. She believed that she had a duty to act on these views—to protest and rally others to protest—to improve society.

Emma Goldman, an uncompromising advocate for individual rights, dedicated her life to fighting government oppression.

Fighting for
Individual Rights

In hundreds of speeches and thousands of writings Goldman presented her ideology of the supreme rights of the individual. She was a pioneer advocate for birth control, equality for women, the eight-hour workday and improvement of other labor conditions, educational reforms, elimination of government control, and unlimited freedom of speech. She also adamantly opposed World War I conscription—the draft, which required men to sign up for military service.

At a time when most women assumed traditional, submissive roles, Emma exercised what she and many others believed was a basic liberty: publicly protesting the injustices she saw in U.S. society. Although she had thousands of loyal supporters and numerous friends throughout her life, Emma's confrontational tactics and radi-

Goldman, shown here speaking with reporters in New York, returned to the United States after she was exiled to Europe for years because of her radical views.

cal views were hated by many others. She was harassed by the press, hounded by the police, and imprisoned. The press called her "America's High Priestess of Anarchism" and "Red Emma." Parents warned their children to behave or they "might grow up to be like Emma Goldman." The U.S. government, always her number-one adversary, ignored its own laws to have her imprisoned.

Deportation

After three decades of skirmishes, U.S. officials finally found a way to silence Goldman—for a time. In 1919, they deported her. But Goldman returned years later to lecture in the United States and Canada with undimmed intensity. Although many thought she would retire in her late sixties, especially after the death of her longtime and beloved comrade, Alexander Berkman, she instead traveled to Europe to deliver speeches and raise funds in support of Spanish anarchists and workers. These Spanish revolutionaries had fought dictatorial rulers in a civil war and had set up farm and industrial collectives,-communities of people who shared ownership of land, buildings, and machinery and voluntarily worked together on their common venture.

Like many others throughout history, Emma Goldman demonstrated in word and deed that an individual acting with courage and conviction can stand up to powerful governments. She never compromised her principles, and her honesty and frankness prompted some who heard or read her views to rethink and challenge ideas and a system that they had not previously questioned. To the end of her life Goldman opposed any form of authority that stifled human development, and championed her ideal society free of repression.

1 Foundations of a Revolutionary

Emma Goldman, the child who would become the person J. Edgar Hoover called the most dangerous woman in America, was born to a desperately poor couple in the rural province of Kovno, Russia (today called Kaunas, in Lithuania), on June 27, 1869. Her humble beginnings could not foretell the heights of notoriety that she would eventually attain as "Red Emma," a label used by the U.S. press associating Emma with the red-and-black flag, the symbol of revolutionaries and radicals of the late 1800s and early 1900s.

Like most poor children born in Russia during the second half of the nineteenth century, Emma Goldman was lucky to survive her early years. Czar Alexander II ruled the country, and a few wealthy farmers and nobles owned the land and ran the government. The peasants, most of whom were illiterate, were barely able to feed and clothe themselves. They had few civil rights—neither the right of free speech nor the right to protest.

Anti-Semitic Discrimination

For Emma's family, life was especially difficult, as it was for all of the Jewish poor. Alexander, who believed that Jews took advantage of non-Jews and prospered on their money, often used the Jews as religious scapegoats. The czar's soldiers and government officials would spread stories about the "evil ones" who had denied Jesus and had him crucified. They would accuse Jews of stealing children and taking part in unholy rituals. Officials warned of

Czar Alexander II, who ruled Russia at the time of Emma's birth, led a repressive regime.

Restricted by the government from farming and many other jobs, Jews in late-nineteenth-century Russia often ended up penniless and on the streets.

the dangers Jews posed if they were allowed to "contaminate" the country with their presence. And, worst of all, they looked the other way when, at frequent intervals, Russian peasants and military men savagely attacked the Jewish population, maiming and killing defenseless people and destroying their property. These organized persecutions, called pogroms, were carried out with the approval, if not the direct order, of Alexander.

The czar also restricted the ways that Jews could make a living. Laws strictly prohibited Jews from farming and from most public service jobs. Most Jews worked in the sweatshops of the clothing trades.

More fortunate Jews eked out an existence by operating small shops and selling basic necessities to their neighbors within the ghetto, a restricted part of a village, town, or city where Jews were required to live.

While all Russians were subject to unfair taxes and demands for bribes from corrupt government bureaucrats, according to Goldman biographer Alix Shulman, Jewish citizens had to "pay special Jewish taxes to the czar and extra bribes to the officials. There were laws restricting whom they could hire, how they could dress, when and where they could travel, where they could build their synagogues, and even when they could marry."[1]

Officially persecuted by their government, Jews were also subjected to anti-Semitism (hostility toward or prejudice against Jews) by the general population. Anti-Semitism was fueled by the Jews' traditional lifestyle, which many non-Jews did not understand and so feared and hated. Biographer Shulman notes that "these solemn, religious people, darker in hair and skin . . . had clung together as a separate people for many generations. . . . Even those Jews who were not religious had kept their own Yiddish language, their own style of dress, and their own ancient customs."[2]

Witnessing Violence

The Goldman family lived within this atmosphere of fear and repression often accompanied by violence. Emma frequently heard stories of peasants being viciously beaten. A beating might be ordered by an employer displeased with the way a peasant worked or behaved, or by a military officer who simply disliked or wished to intimidate the person. In her autobiography, she recalls a day when she was just five years old:

> I came upon a half-naked human body being lashed with the knout [a whip made of intertwined leather strips and wire tied to the end of a long stick]. It threw me into hysterics, and for days I was haunted by the horrible picture . . . : the bleeding body, the piercing shrieks, the distorted faces of the gendarmes [police], the knouts whistling in the air and coming down with a sharp hissing upon the half-naked man.[3]

Emma's mother, Taube, tried to rear her three daughters in a household filled with domestic violence, poverty, and struggle.

This experience and other frightful acts of violence against the poor and helpless were partly responsible for the passion for equality and freedom from oppression she developed later in life.

A Difficult Family Life

Along with brutal social and economic conditions, the Goldmans suffered internal family problems as well. Emma's parents, Taube and Abraham, married after Taube's first husband, Leon Zodikow, died. Taube had two daughters, Helena and Lena, from her first marriage. As was customary at the time, Taube's parents arranged the second marriage. Viewing it as a marriage of convenience and necessity, Taube felt no love for Abraham. Abraham's love for Taube was never returned.

Taube brought a little money to the marriage, but Abraham used it to invest in a business that failed just as Emma was about to be born. Thus Emma's arrival was not greeted with much joy or enthusiasm by her parents. The baby simply became a new mouth to feed, and Abraham Goldman came to resent the extra burden. He could find little love in his heart for his first child.

Before Emma was a year old her family received permission from government officials to move to the village of Popelan, about one hundred miles away on the Russia-Germany border. They lived in Popelan for seven years; there Abraham managed the stagecoach system and ran the nearby inn. Stagecoach travelers, many of them government officials, frequently stayed at the inn.

Brutal Life at the Inn

The inn was the center of the small community's social and political activity, and a tremendous burden for Emma's father and mother. As innkeeper Abraham was under constant pressure to accommodate government officials, who might impulsively decide to have him fired if he did not provide them free food and drink—especially vodka. Even when Abraham tried to gain their favor, officials would make him the butt of jokes or insult him because he was a Jew.

Abraham found himself refereeing almost-nightly drunken brawls besides tending to travelers' needs and caring for their horses. There was so much work that Helena and Lena were also required to spend most of their time keeping up with the chores at the inn. Emma, left to fend for herself during these early chaotic years, became a very lonely but independent child.

Emma's independence brought her into constant conflict with her overworked father. She was by nature and habit outspoken, but as her questions seemed to challenge her father's authority, Abraham believed his daughter was disrespectful. He also thought Emma willful and stubborn because she argued or expressed her own opinions as her siblings did not. Like most fathers of the time, Abraham expected his daughter to be quiet and submissive, to do as she was told without question.

Abraham Goldman vented the pressures of his miserable life on all of his family, screaming and hitting his children for the slightest offenses. But he apparently treated Emma more coldly and more harshly than either of her half-sisters or, after their arrival, her two younger brothers, Herman and Morris. In her autobiography Emma recalls a "ghastly" childhood marked by her father's harshness and violent outbursts. But one of her worst memories was her father "saying that he had not wanted" her.[4]

An Outsider in Her Own Family

Abraham frequently let Emma know that she was unwelcome and almost an interloper in the family. That was the case one day when she came home from school with a report about misbehaving in class. She did not try to hide the report or to make excuses. Instead, she sat gazing out a bay window, waiting for her father's reaction:

Suddenly I felt a terrific pain in my head, as if I had been struck with an iron bar. It was Father's fist that had smashed the round comb I wore to hold my unruly hair. He pounded me and pulled me about, raging: "You are my disgrace! You will always be so! You can't be my child; you don't look like me or like your mother; you don't act like us!"[5]

Emma's father, Abraham, considered Emma a burden on the family and treated her cruelly.

In another incident, Emma remembers her father saying that he'd been cheated by the pig woman because he had not had a boy. This taunt implied that he had negotiated with a pork merchant for the purchase of a male child, but that the woman had tricked him and had given him a girl instead. Since from ancient times Jewish dietary laws have forbidden the eating of pork, the reference to "the pig woman" was particularly scornful and cruel.

Along with such taunts, Emma recalls brutal beatings during this period in her life:

Once Father lashed me with a strap so that my little brother Herman, awakened by my cries, came running up and bit Father on the calf. The lashing stopped. Helena took me to her room, bathed my bruised back, brought me milk, held me to her heart, her tears mingling with mine, while Father outside was raging: "I'll kill her! I'll kill that brat! I will teach her to obey!"[6]

Abraham kept Emma in a near-constant state of fear. She remembers thinking:

Perhaps if I should become very ill, near death, he would become kind and never beat me again or let me stand in the corner for hours, or make me walk back and forth with a glass of water in my hand. "If you spill a drop, you will get whipped!" he would threaten. The whip and the little stool were always at hand. They symbolized my shame and my tragedy. After many attempts and considerable punishment I had learned to carry the glass without spilling a drop of water. The process used to unnerve me and make me ill for hours after.[7]

In spite of her father's outbursts of rage and obvious cruelty, however, Emma craved his attention and approval and she thought him "handsome, dashing, and full of vitality. I loved him even while I was afraid of him. I wanted him to love me, but I never knew how to reach his heart. His hardness only served to make me more contrary."[8]

Emma knew she must someday escape from the abuse of her parents' home. Yet a decade or more later, she learned that her "tragic childhood had been no exception, that there were thousands of children born unwanted, marred and maimed by poverty and still more by ignorant misunderstanding." At this realization Emma determined that "No child of mine should ever be added to those unfortunate victims."[9] She

also vowed to dedicate her life to helping other victims of abuse. But Emma had yet to weather some of her harshest trials.

Early Schooling and More Harsh Discipline

According to her autobiography, Emma was sent at the age of eight to live with her maternal grandmother and attend a Jewish elementary school in Koenigsberg, Germany, where schools were supposedly better than those in Russia. Just one month after beginning her schooling, however, her kindly grandmother was suddenly called away from the village. Emma's uncle, her mother's brother-in-law, took

Children in a German classroom listen attentively to their teacher. Many Russian parents, including Emma's, sent their children to Germany to gain an education.

responsibility for her welfare and the forty rubles a month that her parents sent for her education.

A merciless man, Emma's uncle removed her from school, confiscated her money, and forced her to work as a virtual slave cleaning his house from sunup to sundown. As Emma recalls:

> From early morning, when I had to fetch the rolls, milk, and chocolate for breakfast, until late at night I was kept busy, making beds, cleaning boots, scrubbing floors, and washing clothes. After a while I was even put to cooking, but my uncle was never satisfied.

His gruff voice shouting orders all day long would send cold shivers down my spine. I drudged on. At night I would weep myself to sleep.[10]

Finally a day came when the uncle, returning home to find Emma sitting down to rest after a day of labor, ordered her to deliver a package for him, which would require walking several miles. Emma refused the unreasonable order; enraged, the uncle slapped and kicked her, knocking her down a flight of stairs. Abraham learned about the abuse from another family member, and he hurried to retrieve his daughter.

Emma was terrified to hear that her father was on his way. She was certain that he would be furious with her for creating problems in the family. But Abraham Goldman acted in quite the opposite manner. It was one of the few occasions in Emma's memory that her father actually showed he cared about her. He was so upset by Emma's sickly appearance that he hugged and kissed her for the first time in years.

So Emma returned to Popelan. But a few months later, Abraham lost his position and everything else he had worked for in Popelan. The unfortunate family had no place to live, so they relocated near Taube's family in Koenigsberg. And Emma returned to school once more.

Over the next four years, Emma completed sufficient course work to undertake the tough entrance examination for the German gymnasium (high school). She worked hard to pass, but to qualify for enrollment in gymnasium she also had to have a certificate from her religion teacher attesting to her good character.

Emma's Love for Children

Early in her life Emma expressed a love of young children, and at one time hoped to rear her own. As she writes in her autobiography, Living My Life:

"As a little girl I used to look with envious eyes on the strange little babies our neighbour's daughter played with, dressing them up and putting them to sleep. I was told they were not real babies, they were only dolls, although to me they were living things because they were so beautiful. I longed for dolls, but I never had any.

When my brother Herman was born, I was only four years old. He replaced the need of dolls in my life. The arrival of little Leibale [Morris] two years later filled me with ecstatic joy. I was always near him, rocking and singing him to sleep. Once when he was about a year old, Mother put him in my bed. After she left, the child began to cry. He must be hungry, I thought. I remembered how Mother gave him the breast. I, too, would give him my breast. I picked him up in my arms and pressed his little mouth close to me, rocking and cooing and urging him to drink. Instead he began to choke, turned blue in the face, and gasped for breath. Mother came running in and demanded to know what I had done to Baby. I explained. She broke out into laughter, then slapped and scolded me. I wept, not from pain, but because my breast had no milk for Leibale."

Emma "loathed the idea of asking the man for anything." She viewed her teacher as a hypocrite because of his overbearing attitude and rigid discipline, which included frequent whippings. Emma believed that these characteristics were inconsistent in a truly religious person. As a result she had no respect for his authority, joining classmates in harassing him with pranks—placing tacks on his chair and sticking snails in his pockets. Nevertheless Emma had to ask for her certificate of character.

> I felt my whole future depended on it . . . [but] in front of the whole class he announced that he would never give me a good character. I had none, he declared: I was a terrible child and would grow into a worse woman. . . . I would surely end on the public gallows as a public menace. I went home heart-broken.[11]

Soon after this the family left Germany and in the winter of 1881 moved back to Russia and the Jewish ghetto in the capital, Saint Petersburg, where Abraham had been given an opportunity to manage a cousin's dry-goods store.

The Influence of Nihilist Thinking

In Saint Petersburg in 1882, when Emma was thirteen, she attended a Russian school for what proved to be her last six months of formal education. During those six months, however, she came into contact with radical students, who often talked about Russian officials who beat peasants and arrested, imprisoned, and tortured people who protested against the government. One particular radical movement, the Nihilists, was gaining popularity at the time.

The Nihilists were activists who believed that the monarchy was to blame for all of the ills of Russian society, and who advocated revolution, violent if necessary. A year before Emma returned to Saint Petersburg, some of these radicals had murdered Alexander. In the activists' view, the assassination was justified because existing

Police arrest a suspected Nihilist in Saint Petersburg. The ideas of the popular Nihilist movement in Russia intrigued Emma from a young age.

conditions were so bad that destruction of the social order was a good thing for its own sake. However, the new czar, Alexander III, became even more repressive, reducing individual freedoms even further.

Emma's mother, Taube, had railed against the Nihilist assassins, declaring that "they ought to be exterminated, everyone of them!"[12] Indeed, the radicals who killed the czar were caught and hanged, but Emma did not share her mother's belief that justice had been served. Instead she accepted a view expressed by some of her classmates and teachers, who were sympathetic toward the assassins and believed their act, though violent, showed that people would stand up against oppressors.

Although she was too young to understand radical Nihilist theories, "the seeds of rebellion and unrelenting hatred of oppression were . . . planted in the heart of Emma Goldman," notes Hippolyte Havel in a biographical sketch written years later. Havel explains that early in her life Emma "saw her father harassed" by government officials, and "beheld the young [Jewish] men, often the sole support of a large family, brutally dragged to the barracks to lead the miserable life of a soldier."[13] (During this period, Russian officials frequently kidnapped Jewish boys, some as young as twelve years old, to serve in the military.)

"My Guiding Stars"

At an early age Emma also read Russian novels in which heroic characters were Nihilists, and she studied the real-life events surrounding the courageous revolutionary

Revolutionary Vera Zasulich (pictured) tried to assassinate the unjust governor of Saint Petersburg in 1878. Emma, who was nine years old at the time, saw Zasulich as a courageous heroine.

Vera Zasulich, who had tried to kill the repressive governor of Saint Petersburg in 1878. The young woman's act greatly influenced Emma, who saw Zasulich as a heroine, willing to give up her own freedom to rid her people of a cruel dictator. "The Nihilists . . . became to me heroes and martyrs, henceforth my guiding stars," Emma writes in her autobiography.[14]

Emma was soon forced to quit school when her father lost his job again. She found tedious, mind-numbing work at a corset factory in the city, but she spent every night in her room reading about the heroines and heroes of her newfound cause: fighting repressive authority in all its guises. She found she could no longer tolerate the abuses of her father or the traditional customs and systems that supported such behavior.

Her father would discover this soon enough. Never comfortable with his troublesome daughter's defiance and certain that she had "loose morals" that would lead her to a life of prostitution, Abraham arranged for Emma's marriage when she was fifteen years old. Emma wanted no part of it. But no matter how much she begged, reasoned, and cried, her father would not be swayed. Emma became desperate. She knew that her father had the legal power to force her to marry anyone he chose. Such practice was in fact com-

Going to the Opera

Emma first began to appreciate music and drama at the age of ten, when one of her teachers, who rejected traditional instruction and wanted to enlighten her pupils with music and literature, took Emma to hear the opera Il Trovatore. *She describes the experience in* Living My Life.

"My teacher may have been largely responsible for the electrifying effect of that experience: she had imbued me with the romance of her favourite German authors and had helped to rouse my imagination. . . . The tortuous suspense of the days before Mother gave her consent to my accompanying my teacher to the performance aggravated my tense expectancy. We reached the Opera a full hour before the beginning, myself in a cold sweat for fear we were late. Teacher, always in delicate health, could not keep up with my young legs and my frenzied haste to reach our places. I flew up to the top gallery, three steps at a time. The house was still empty and half-lit, and somewhat disappointing at first. As if by magic, it soon became transformed. Quickly the place filled with a vast audience—women in silks and velvets of gorgeous hue, with glistening jewels on their bare necks and arms, the flood of light from the crystal chandeliers reflecting the colours of green, yellow, and amethyst. It was a fairyland more magnificent than any ever pictured in the stories I had read. I forgot the presence of my teacher, the mean surroundings of my home; half-hanging over the rail, I was lost in the enchanted world below. The orchestra broke into stirring tones, mysteriously rising from the darkened house. They sent tremors down my back and held me breathless by their swelling sounds."

Immigrants to the United States get their first glimpse of the Statue of Liberty as they sail into New York Harbor. Emma left her home in Russia to make the same journey in 1885.

mon: In 1884 females had only the rights that their fathers, then their husbands, allowed them.

Emma had to act decisively. Her half-sister Helena had planned to join Lena, who had already made a life in America, and now Emma threatened to commit suicide if she were not allowed to leave too. One thing that Abraham Goldman had learned about his daughter was that, once decided, he could not change her mind. He feared that she might actually throw herself into the river to drown. Helena offered to pay Emma's passage on the ship to America, and finally Abraham agreed to let her go. In December 1885, the same year the Statue of Liberty was erected in New York Harbor, the sixteen-year-old Emma Goldman ended her childhood and set sail for the United States.

2 Coming of Age in America

The last day of our journey comes vividly to mind. Everybody was on deck. Helena and I stood pressed to each other, enraptured by the sight of the harbour and the Statue of Liberty suddenly emerging from the mist. Ah, there she was, the symbol of hope, of freedom, of opportunity! She held her torch high to light the way to the free country, the asylum for the oppressed of all lands. We, too, Helena and I, would find a place in the generous heart of America. Our spirits were high, our eyes filled with tears.[15]

So Emma recalls her feelings as she steamed into New York Harbor with grand expectations about life in her new land. Her excitement soon turned to dismay, however, as she and Helena were forced through the confusing and dehumanizing immigration process that took place in the

Immigrants shuffle through the mazelike immigration building at New York Harbor upon their arrival in the United States. For many of those coming to America, getting through the confusing and dehumanizing immigration process was the first hurdle to what they hoped was a better life.

site known as Castle Garden, Ellis Island. Here, she remembers, "the atmosphere was charged with antagonism and harshness. Nowhere could one see a sympathetic official face; there was no provision for the comfort of the new arrivals, the pregnant women and young children."[16]

Goldman's impressions of America did not get much better during that first cold January in 1886, when she and Helena finally reached Rochester, New York, and the Jewish neighborhood where their sister Lena lived. Lena and her husband, who were expecting their first child, provided a small, clean room for the two sisters. But Emma and Helena soon realized that their presence would be a burden on the young family, even though Lena was very happy to see her sisters and to hear news of home.

"Lena told us how lonely she had been," writes Emma, "how she had longed for us and for our people. We learned of the hard life that had been hers." And although Lena was thrilled about the arrival of her first child, "'Life is still difficult,' she said; 'my husband is earning twelve dollars a week as a tinsmith, working on roofs in the beating sun and in the cold wind, always in danger.'"[17] Emma and Helena vowed to find employment at once to pay their share of expenses.

Factory Work and Marriage

When she lived in Russia, Emma was trained as a glove maker. She also had experience knitting shawls. So she had little difficulty finding factory work at the Garson and Mayer Company in Rochester, where she was hired to make ulsters, long, loose overcoats of rough cloth.

Goldman's older sisters, Lena (left) and Helena (right), helped Emma adjust to her new life in America.

At Garson and Mayer, workers were watched constantly and prodded to work faster if they paused to rest or to have a word with one another. "The amazing thing to me," writes Emma, "was that no one else in the factory seemed to be so affected as I."[18]

Emma worked ten and a half hours a day and was paid $2.50 a week. Of this she gave $1.50 to Lena for board, spent 60 cents on carfare to work, and kept 40 cents. After the birth of Lena's daughter, Emma realized that she would need more money to help ease her sister's financial burden, so she asked Mr. Garson for a raise. She explained that the wage she and the other workers received was simply not enough to pay for the basic necessities of life, let alone the occasional 25-cent theater ticket or book.

*Working conditions in the late nineteenth century were often deplorable.
Laborers, who worked long hours for little pay, were reluctant to complain for
fear of losing their jobs.*

Garson's reaction was abrupt and final: "If I raise your wages, I'll have to raise the others' as well and I can't afford that."[19] He suggested that Emma was extravagant and told her she should be happy with what he paid her. But Emma was not satisfied; a few days later she found a job working for Rubinstein's factory, which was closer to home and offered to pay $4.00 a week.

Working beside her at Rubinstein's was a young coat maker named Jacob Kershner. Jacob was from Russia too, arriving in America from Odessa in 1881. The two found that they had much in common and lived near each other. Soon they were walking to and from work together and socializing when they could find time after work. Emma writes:

I had known Jacob Kershner about four months when he asked me to marry him. I admitted I liked him, but I did not want to marry so young. We still knew so little of each other. He said that he'd wait as long as I pleased, but there was already a great deal of talk about our being out together so much.[20]

Emma resisted the idea of marriage for a little while, but she was lonely. She accepted Jacob's proposal, and in 1887 they were wed, in accordance with Jewish law, by a rabbi in Rochester.

The Labor Movement

Emma had arrived in the United States during a period of dramatic social change. She went to work in an American factory just as an industrial revolution was under way in the United States. Industries were expanding and factories needed workers, and a glut of people were available to fill the jobs. Many rural Americans left farms and moved to cities to work in factories at the same time as millions of European immigrants came to the United States and settled in urban areas, where they eagerly sought work. Employers could easily replace any workers who did not accept the low wages offered for a twelve- to fourteen-hour workday or who complained about working conditions, which often presented health and safety hazards.

In a literal sense, the owners of such big businesses as manufacturing plants, railroads, and coal mines were dictators. They set unregulated hiring policies; they determined the hours laborers worked and the amount they were paid according to no standard but their own. And they refused to spend money for protective measures

Venting Anger

Because of growing anti-Semitism in Russia, Goldman's parents immigrated to America in 1886 and went to live in Rochester, New York, in a household that included Emma, her half-sister Helena, and her two brothers. Emma soon married Jacob Kershner, in part to escape what she felt were her father's efforts to enchain her. After she left Kershner, she also broke away from her father. In her autobiography, Living My Life, *Goldman describes the scene.*

"Mother had not been feeling well and I went over to put her house in order. I was on the floor scrubbing while Father was nagging me for having married Kershner, for having left him, and again for returning to him. 'You are a loose character,' he kept on saying; 'you have always disgraced yourself in the family.' He talked, while I continued scrubbing.

Then something snapped within me; my lone and woeful childhood, my tormented adolescence, my joyless youth—I flung them all into Father's face. He stood aghast as I denounced him, emphasizing every charge by beating my scrubbing-brush on the floor. Every cruel incident of my life stood out in my arraignment. Our large barn of a home, Father's angry voice resounding through it, his ill-treatment of the servants, his iron grip on my mother—everything that had haunted my days and terrorized my nights I now recalled in my bitterness. . . . It was Helena's love and devotion that had saved me.

My words rushed on like a torrent, the brush pounding the floor with all the hatred and scorn I felt for my father. The terrible scene ended with my hysterical screams. My brothers carried me up and put me to bed. The next morning I left the house."

(such as improved lighting and ventilation) to safeguard the health and safety of workers. Working-class people had little if any power or freedom to protest, because government officials at the federal, state, and local levels enacted laws that favored business owners. As a result, big business owners amassed huge fortunes; they controlled the means of production, both resources and labor, and thus most of the wealth.

Reacting to this abuse of power, workers began to organize and form associations (or unions) and to strike—they quit working until their demands for shorter working hours, higher wages, and improved working conditions were met. However, industrialists often punished striking workers with what they called a "rifle diet," hiring people to break up strikes with gunfire. Some industrialists bragged that they could "hire half the working class to shoot the other half," because they knew so many people needed jobs.[21]

One of the labor groups organized in the United States was the International Working People's Association (IWPA), founded by German immigrants who were socialists and anarchists. Socialists basically believed that all property and means of production should be collectively or government owned and that a central government under the control of workers should administer the distribution of goods; they advocated education and political action to achieve their goals. Anarchists emphasized individual liberty and opposed all organized government as repressive; many thought violent revolution was the only way to eliminate authority. These differences were put aside, however, when the IWPA joined other U.S. workers' unions to demand an eight-hour workday. Thousands of laborers across the United States demonstrated for the eight-hour day, and in the spring of 1886 workers in Chicago staged a series of strikes to support it.

One of the strikes was against the McCormick Reaper Works, which manufactured harvesting machines. On May 3, 1886, August Spies, an anarchist, was addressing strikers outside the factory when "scabs," or strikebreakers who had been hired to take the place of striking workers, left the factory. According to one account, "A pitched battle ensued. The police were called, and when they were assaulted with stones, they opened fire on the crowd, shooting indiscriminately men, women, and children, killing six and wounding many more."[22]

The Haymarket Riot

Shocked workers and their supporters called for a rally the next day to protest the police brutality. Hundreds gathered at Haymarket Square in Chicago, and by all accounts the meeting was peaceful. But when police units arrived to disperse the crowd, someone threw a dynamite bomb into their ranks. Gunfire broke out between the workers and the police. In the end, seven policemen were killed and sixty others in the square were injured.

The citizens of Chicago were outraged, and the press blamed anarchists for the tragedy. Leaders of the IWPA and other labor organizations were rounded up. Eight anarchists, among them August Spies, were tried and convicted of conspiracy to commit murder, although there was no proof that the anarchists had aided the bomber and no one could identify the culprit. Seven of the radical activists were sen-

A dynamite bomb suddenly explodes among police at a rally at Haymarket Square. The resulting riot ended in the death of seven police officers.

tenced to die by hanging, and the eighth was sentenced to fifteen years in prison. Some prominent lawyers at the time protested that the men had been found guilty because of their political convictions and that the trial and sentencing were a mockery of justice. As the condemned August Spies stated:

> If we cannot be directly implicated with this affair, connected with the throwing of the bomb, where is the law that says "that these men shall be picked out to suffer"? Show me that law if you have it. If the position of this court is correct, then half of this city—

half of the population of this city—ought to be hanged, because they are responsible the same as we are for that act on May 4th. . . . Your decision, your verdict, our conviction is nothing but an arbitrary will of this lawless court.[23]

The governor of Illinois eventually reduced the death sentences of two of the convicted men to life imprisonment, and another killed himself in prison. Then more than a year after the trial, on November 11, 1887, the four remaining activists were executed in Illinois. Before he died, August Spies shouted defiantly: "If you think that by hanging us you can stamp

Anarchist August Spies sits in a Chicago jail cell after being convicted of conspiracy to commit murder at Haymarket Square.

out the labor movement—the movement from which the downtrodden millions who toil and live in want and misery . . . expect salvation—if this is your opinion then hang us! Here you will tread upon a spark, but . . . flames will blaze up."[24]

"Too Horrible Even for Tears"

Emma had read whatever news she could find about the Haymarket case, and she agreed with those who defended the anarchists. She was convinced that the government had made examples of the eight men and wanted to show what could happen to people who did not follow the dictates of the state. To Emma, this was no different from the kind of oppressive government she had known in Russia. She was also deeply impressed by the fact that the condemned men had fought against injustice and faced death because of their beliefs.

Four convicted anarchists, including August Spies, face death by hanging. Goldman sympathized with the anarchists and felt they were wrongly executed.

In The German-Americans: An Informal History, *Richard O'Connor points out that anarchist theories were prevalent among German immigrants in Chicago during the 1870s and 1880s. They often read anarchist newspapers, one of which was edited by August Spies.*

"Jobs had become scarce as a result of the depression of '73 and there was great economic pressure on both the immigrant and the longer established families. Few of the newcomers spoke English but most could make themselves understood in German. . . . Seeking distraction from their troubles, they had to find places where German was spoken. . . .

The seeds of . . . agitation, in print and on the platform, fell upon fertile ground. No one else seemed to be concerned with the plight of Chicago's unemployed immigrants, most of them German or German-speaking. . . .

There were no voices of moderation speaking in a language the immigrants could understand."

When the news of the hangings reached Emma and Helena in Rochester, they "were crushed. . . . The shock completely unnerved my sister; she could only wring her hands and weep silently," Emma writes. "I was in a stupor; a feeling of numbness came over me, something too horrible even for tears." Emma and Helena went to the home of their father, who had recently followed his daughters to Rochester. As Emma recalls:

Everybody talked about the Chicago events. I was entirely absorbed in what I felt as my own loss. Then I heard the coarse laugh of a woman. In a shrill voice she sneered: "What's all this lament about? The men were murderers. It is well they were hanged." With one leap I was at the woman's throat. Then I felt myself torn back. Someone said: "The child has gone crazy." I wrenched myself free, grabbed a pitcher of water from the table, and threw it with all my force into the woman's face. "Out, out," I cried, "or I will kill you!" The terrified woman made for the door and I dropped to the ground in a fit of crying. I was put to bed, and soon fell into a deep sleep. The next morning I woke as from a long illness. . . . I had a distinct sensation that something new and wonderful had been born in my soul. A great ideal, a burning faith, a determination to dedicate myself to [the Haymarket martyrs], to make their cause my own, to make known to the world their beautiful lives and heroic deaths.[25]

Clearly, the Haymarket events had a profound effect on Emma, and her views became ever more radical. There was little doubt that she believed in anarchism, which she later defined, in part, as "the theory that all forms of government rest on violence, and are therefore wrong and harmful, as well as unnecessary."[26]

An Unhappy Marriage

As Emma was crystallizing her views on anarchy, she was also trying to deal with misgivings about her marriage. Not long after she married Jacob Kershner, Emma realized that she was far too different from her new husband for the marriage to work. While he was content to join the other male factory workers in card games and activities she considered frivolous, Emma yearned for the stimulating life she had known in Saint Petersburg: "living in the world of books I had read, the operas I had heard, the circle of students I had known."[27]

Emma still liked Jacob, but became increasingly unhappy with her life in Rochester. At her insistence, Jacob gave her a divorce. Emma then moved to New Haven, Connecticut, to work in a corset factory, but the long hours adversely affected her health and she was forced to return to Rochester.

There Jacob begged her to come back to him and remarry, threatening to kill himself if she refused. He actually showed her the agent—a bottle of poison. Emma did not want the desperate man to harm himself, so she reluctantly agreed to remarry. But, she writes: "I was not naive enough to think that a renewed life with Kershner would prove more satisfactory or lasting than at first. Besides, I had definitely decided to go to New York [City]."[28]

The Anarchist Life

The Haymarket incident had inspired Emma and given her life new meaning. She decided to follow through on her vow to make the cause of the Haymarket men her own. Her family and members of the Jewish community in Rochester were openly critical of Emma's decision, calling her wicked and otherwise insulting her. But in 1889 she left Jacob Kershner once more and moved to New York City. After all, it was in New York where anarchist thought and action were most prominent. There great thinkers and orators were dedicating their lives to the creation of a just society. Emma was sure she would find the truth she was seeking—the anarchist answer. Jacob stayed in Rochester a short time after Emma left, but then he mysteriously disappeared. According to reports years later, he apparently stole money from a social club and served a prison term for the crime.

During this time the U.S. anarchist movement was becoming more sharply defined. The New York anarchists, like the socialists and anarchists in Chicago, had found that their greatest influence was within the labor movement, especially among workers who had recently emigrated from Russia, Poland, and Germany. The foremost leader of this movement was the charismatic Johann Most, who published a German-language anarchist paper, *Die Freiheit* (*Freedom*). Emma had read his writings for months, particularly his articles defending the condemned Chicago anarchists. And she had come to believe that his attacks on the cruel capitalist power structure were right on target.

No Turning Back

Goldman stepped off the Weehawken ferry in New York City on August 15, 1889, at the age of twenty. She checked her sewing machine at the baggage room and set off on foot with a few articles of clothing and $5.00 in her pocket, looking for an aunt and uncle who owned a photography shop in the city. Three hours later she found her relatives, but they greeted her coolly, so, even though she was very tired, she decided to move on to search for a political acquaintance, known as A. Solotaroff. She had met Solotaroff following a lecture on anarchy he had delivered while Goldman was in New Haven.

After an extensive search, she found Solotaroff, who greeted her enthusiastically and took her to Sach's Cafe on the Lower East Side of New York City. Once inside the café, Emma knew why she had come to New York City. The loud and friendly establishment was *the* place for radicals to meet. Everywhere one could hear Russian being spoken. All the patrons seemed passionate and animated. Ideas and debate flourished. In short, Emma felt she had found a real home.

Anarchist Johann Most delivers a fiery speech to a group of supporters in New York City. Goldman shared the charismatic leader's radical views against the capitalist power structure.

Goldman found she had much in common with anarchist Alexander Berkman, and the two agreed to work together to fight for their cause.

In the days that followed, Solotaroff helped her find a room to rent with Helen and Anna Minkin, sisters who were Emma's age. Once settled Emma resumed regular visits to Sach's, where she soon met Alexander Berkman, a young anarchist agitator. Though put off by Berkman's rough manner and intensity at the beginning, Emma discovered that they had much in common. After one long evening of walking and talking, Emma remembers:

It was late in the evening when we parted. Berkman had told me little about himself, except that he had been expelled from Gymnasium for an anti-religious essay he had composed, and that he had left home for good. He had come to the United States in the belief that it was free and that here everyone had an equal chance in life. He knew better now. He had found exploitation more severe, and since the hanging of the Chicago anarchists he had become convinced that America was as despotic as Russia.

"Lingg [one of the Haymarket anarchists] was right when he said: 'If you attack us with cannon, we will reply with dynamite.' Someday I will avenge our dead," he added with great earnestness. "I too! I too!" I cried; "their death gave me life. It now belongs to their memory—to their work." He gripped my arm until it hurt. "We are comrades. Let us be friends, too—let us work together." His intensity vibrated through me as I walked up the stairs to the Minkin flat.[29]

Chapter

3 Dedicated to "the Cause"

Alexander Berkman was pleasantly surprised to find that so young a woman as Emma Goldman was well read and dedicated to the anarchist philosophy. He had decided to devote his life to "the cause," and, in his obsession, could tolerate nothing less from those around him. In Goldman he sensed a kindred spirit. The longer they were together, the closer they became. Goldman recalls his words: "We have much in common, haven't we? We even come from the same city. Do you know that Kovno has given many brave sons to the revolutionary movement? And now perhaps a brave daughter." Goldman was embarrassed at the recognition she was receiving from Berkman. "I felt myself turn red. My soul was so proud. 'I hope I shall not fail when the time comes,' I replied."[30]

The Meeting with Most

Berkman decided to take Goldman to meet the anarchist leader Johann Most, publisher of *Die Freiheit*. It was the highest compliment Berkman could have paid her, but the idea of meeting Johann Most was awesome and somewhat intimidating. Goldman had held the revolutionary leader in high esteem since her days in Rochester, when his writings were the only thing that seemed to make sense in a world bent on cruelty and inequality.

Goldman decided at a young age to dedicate herself to anarchist principles.

When Goldman and Most came face-to-face, she could barely speak. But Most was positively impressed by the young woman who had come to learn about the revolution at his feet. During several intimate meetings that followed, they shared their thoughts about the movement, and Goldman expressed her desire to help in whatever he was planning.

Johann Most promised to teach her what he could. Even though, as Goldman notes:

> He didn't believe much in woman's revolutionary zeal. But I, coming from Russia, might be different and he would help me. If I were really in earnest, I could find much work to do. "There is great need in our ranks of . . . young, willing people—ardent ones, as you seem to be—and I have need of ardent friendship," he added with much feeling.[31]

Most's confession of loneliness surprised Goldman. She had thought that anyone of such great renown would never lack for friendship. But Most was not an easy man to like. Even those who were sympathetic to his ideas often found him to be a bully and an intolerant taskmaster. And then there was his appearance. As Emma writes in her autobiography, "My first impression of him was of revulsion. He was of medium height, with a large head crowned with greyish bushy hair; but his face was twisted out of form by an apparent dislocation of the left jaw. Only his eyes were soothing; they were blue and sympathetic."[32]

Most's face had been deformed when a jaw infection in early childhood was not properly treated. Goldman learned that this disfigurement had prevented him from becoming the actor he had always wanted to be. Yet he had found a way to perform: his speeches and his writings were dramatic expressions of a different sort. His political philosophy developed partly because he had been shunned for years by so-called normal people who were repulsed by his contorted looks. Goldman wanted to help her hero, and he soon suggested a way. But first she had to get a job.

Becoming a Spokeswoman

Goldman found a factory job working with Helen Minkin, but she soon had to quit because she did not have the strength to work the long, grueling hours. Besides, she felt such work was a waste of time she should spend reading the books that Most and Berkman were obtaining for her. She eventually set up a sewing business out of her apartment, which allowed her to dedicate more of her time to the cause.

Over a period of six months, Most discovered that his young protégée had a rare talent for oratory. One night in a café, Goldman had told him the story of her experiences in Russia, and the old man was spellbound. He decided at that moment that she should go out on the road to lecture the masses on the themes and ideas he thought were most important. He would train her "to take my place when I am gone."[33]

Most quickly arranged a two-week speaking tour that would eventually take Goldman to Cleveland, Ohio, but her first speech was to be delivered in Rochester, New York. Goldman protested. The prospect of getting up to address a large crowd was frightening enough, so why

A pen-and-ink drawing depicts Goldman speaking at a New York café. When Most discovered Goldman's talent for oratory he immediately encouraged her to become a spokeswoman for the anarchist movement.

agreed to support her in becoming a spokeswoman for the movement. After all, no woman had ever launched a national speaking tour on anarchist ideas. They were all very excited about the prospect.

Goldman quit her sewing work and her companions took over her domestic chores. She had much to learn before the day came to travel back to Rochester. Johann Most had assigned her a speech on the futile struggle for an eight-hour workday. Although Most supported limits on the workday—the issue that had led to the deaths of the Chicago anarchists—he theorized that this issue was secondary to the basic message of anarchism. Most believed that focusing on this particular issue would distract the masses from the goal of establishing a new society that eliminated capitalism entirely.

Goldman read a great deal of anarchist philosophy but doubted that she could present ideas as convincingly as Most did. But Most insisted that all Goldman had to do was memorize the notes he gave her. As she recalls, "He was sure that my dramatic feeling and my enthusiasm would do the rest."[34]

make it worse by giving her first speech in a city she felt was already hostile to her? She was distraught for weeks. However, Most wanted her to go ahead with the plan, and her friends and Berkman were thrilled for her, so she agreed to try her best.

Goldman had moved to a new apartment, which she shared with Helen Minkin, Alexander Berkman, and Berkman's cousin Fedya, an artistic and gentle man whom Goldman could not help but love. She also could not help loving Sasha, her pet name for Berkman. The four roommates were all dedicated to the success of the revolution, so they had little time for jealousy over personal relationships, and simply accepted the fact that Goldman loved two men. They also

Return to Rochester

Helena met with Emma soon after she arrived in Rochester, and Emma told her sister about the speech she was to deliver the next day. Helena, absolutely aghast, protested strongly, warning that the speech would harm their parents and that Emma couldn't possibly be ready to address a large audience after such a brief time away. But Emma would not be dissuaded. She had never been angry with

Importance of the Written Word

Goldman believed the "spoken word hurled forth among the masses with such wonderful eloquence, such enthusiasm and fire, could never be erased from the human mind and soul." But she later realized that lectures and speeches had limitations and that, she explains in Living My Life, *it was important also to publish her ideas.*

"Oral propaganda is at best but a means of shaking people from their lethargy: it leaves no lasting impression. The very fact that most people attend meetings only if aroused by newspaper sensations, or because they expect to be amused, is proof that they really have no inner urge to learn. . . .

In meetings the audience is distracted by a thousand nonessentials. The speaker, though ever so eloquent, cannot escape the restlessness of the crowd, with the inevitable result that he will fail to strike root. In all probability he will not even do justice to himself.

The relation between the writer and the readers is more intimate. True, books are only what we want them to be; rather, what we read into them. That we can do so demonstrates the importance of written as against oral expression."

her sister before, but now she lost her temper. Why couldn't Helena see that Emma was embarking on a new life? Emma scolded Helena for allowing their parents to run her life. That, Emma said, would not happen to her.

In spite of their disagreement, the sisters parted as friends. Helena came to believe that Emma was doing the right thing, and she was especially impressed with Emma's powers of persuasion, predicting that Emma would be a success. But Emma was uncertain.

When I faced the audience the next evening, my mind was blank. I could not remember a single word of my notes. I shut my eyes for an instant; then something strange happened. In a flash I saw it—every incident of my three years in Rochester: the Garson factory, its drudgery and humiliation, the failure of my marriage, the Chicago crime. The last words of August Spies rang in my ears: "Our silence will speak louder than the voices you strangle today."

I began to speak. Words I had never heard myself utter before came pouring forth, faster and faster. They came with passionate intensity; they painted images of the heroic men on the gallows, their glowing vision of an ideal life, rich with comfort and beauty: men and women radiant with freedom, children transformed by joy and affection. The audience had vanished, the hall itself had disappeared; I was conscious only of my own words, of my ecstatic song.

I stopped. Tumultuous applause rolled over me, the buzzing of voices, people telling me something I could not understand. Then I heard someone quite close to me: "It was an inspired speech; but what about the eight-hour struggle? You've said nothing about that." I felt hurled down from my exalted heights, crushed. I told the chairman I was too tired to answer questions, and I went home feeling ill in body and mind. I let myself quietly into Helena's apartment and threw myself on the bed in my clothes.[35]

Goldman had mixed emotions about her first speech. She realized she could sway an audience, but she had not conveyed Most's message that the struggle for the eight-hour workday wasted time and energy and would achieve only temporary gains. She tried a different approach in Buffalo the next day and also in Cleveland a few days later, urging workers to look to the future and the overthrow of the capitalist system.

But after her Cleveland speech a man with white hair sitting in the front row got up to speak. As Goldman reports:

He said that he understood my impatience with such small demands as a few hours less [work] a day, or a few

Activists try to convince workers to join their fight for the eight-hour workday. Goldman, who originally saw the struggle for the shorter workday as trivial, changed her view when she realized how strongly many workers felt about the issue.

dollars more [pay] a week. It was legitimate for young people to take time lightly. But what were men of his age to do? They were not likely to live to see the ultimate overthrow of the capitalist system. Were they also to forgo the release of perhaps two hours a day from the hated work? . . . Should they deny themselves even that small achievement? Should they never have a little more time for reading or being out in the open? Why not be fair to people chained to the block?[36]

When the elderly man finished speaking, Goldman understood more clearly how meaningful the struggle for the eight-hour workday was to the ordinary worker. She reports that the man's words "brought home to me the falsity of Most's position. I realized I was committing a crime against myself and the workers by serving as a parrot repeating Most's views."[37]

Goldman returned to New York from her first speaking tour pleased with a new-found confidence in her speaking abilities, but uncertain how to tell Most about her changed perspective, which no longer matched that of her mentor. Most was concerned with the greater goal of revolutionizing the economic and political system; Goldman, as she would do through most of her life, related the cause to its practical application in the daily affairs of real people. She could not ignore the plight of workers who were suffering even as she spoke of abstract ideals.

The following evening Goldman met Most at a café:

He joined me in a gay mood, presenting me with a large bouquet of violets. The two weeks of my absence had been unbearably long, he said, and he reproached himself for having let me go just when we had grown so close. But now he would never again let me go—not alone, anyhow.

I tried several times to tell him about my trip . . . was he not interested in whether or not I had proved an apt pupil? "Yes, another time." Now he wanted only to feel me near—his Blondkopf, his little girl-woman.

I flared up, declaring I would not be treated as a mere female. I blurted out that I would never again follow blindly, that I had made a fool of myself.[38]

Most did not react to Goldman's outburst until he had paid the bill and they had left the café. Then, as Goldman writes:

He burst into a storm of abuse. He had reared a viper, a snake, a heartless coquette, who had played with him like a cat with a mouse. He had sent me out to plead his cause and I had betrayed him. I was like the rest, but he would not stand for it. He would rather cut me out of his heart right now than have me as a lukewarm friend. "Who is not with me is against me," he shouted; "I will not have it otherwise!"[39]

Defining Anarchism

Goldman could not believe that an anarchist like Most, whose highest ideals were individual liberty and the absolute right to express personal opinions, would make such a statement. But in spite of his reaction, she continued to work with him.

Though his anarchist philosophies were not identical to Goldman's, Most acted as Goldman's mentor.

Meanwhile she pursued her own brand of anarchism, one that acknowledged a place for aesthetics and the arts within the movement. Anarchists like Most and Berkman always ranted about placing the cause before all else in life, but Goldman believed anarchism would best be embodied in individuals with the freedom to follow varied interests and such creative outlets as music, dance, and literature. She vowed to become an example of what true anarchism could achieve.

Once Goldman was criticized for enjoying herself too much at a dance. "It was undignified for one who was on the way to become a force in the anarchist movement," she was told by a young cousin of Berkman. But Goldman loved to dance, and she

grew furious with the impudent interference of the boy. I told him to mind his own business. . . . "I want freedom, the right to self-expression, everybody's right to beautiful, radiant things." Anarchism meant that to me, and I would live it in spite of the whole world—prisons, persecution, everything. Yes, even in spite of the condemnation of my own closest comrades I would live my beautiful ideal.[40]

As she continued to develop her philosophy and to hone her speaking and writing skills, Goldman and her small commune made several moves in search of jobs that would help pay their expenses while they worked for the anarchist cause. In 1892 Emma, Sasha, and Fedya moved to Worcester, Massachusetts, where they opened an ice cream parlor. They hoped to earn enough money to send Berkman back to Russia, where he could work for a rebellion against the czar.

But before they could carry out their plan, they heard news of a strike at the Carnegie Steel Company plant in Homestead, Pennsylvania. Henry Clay Frick, chairman of the board of Carnegie Steel, had threatened to call in the Pinkerton Detective Agency. The Pinkerton agency was the first of numerous businesses set up in the late 1800s that hired out armed men to industrialists. Some employees were simply paid thugs—former thieves, murderers, or other criminals who, for a price, were willing to do whatever their employers asked—legal or not.

Goldman and Berkman determined that the time was now ripe for "the awakening of the American worker, the long-awaited day of his resurrection."[41] They

When head of the Carnegie Steel Company Henry Clay Frick attempted to cut wages, hundreds of Pennyslvania steelworkers went on strike to protest.

scale, and the workers went on strike in protest.

Henry Frick was a prime example of the industrial capitalist of the late nineteenth century. Like Andrew Carnegie, J. P. Morgan, and John D. Rockefeller, Frick was a "captain of commerce" who exerted tight control over natural resources, the means of production, government regulations, and ultimately the lives of the common working class. Industrialists believed that labor unions just got in the way of production and, therefore, profits.

Frick notified Robert Pinkerton to send three hundred guards to the steelworks to take control of the plant so that Frick could hire new workers and continue to produce steel. Dubbed "Fort Frick," the steel plant was located on a river and surrounded by a barbed-wire fence fifteen feet high and three miles long.

Meanwhile, Berkman and Goldman were trying to produce a pamphlet on labor issues and distribute it among the protesters at Homestead. But early in the morning of July 6 the Pinkertons arrived by boat, landing at the plant. According to one published account:

closed down the ice cream parlor and returned to New York City to organize in support of the Pennsylvania workers.

The Homestead Strike

The labor union that represented the Carnegie workers was the conservative Amalgamated Association of Iron and Steel Workers. Their contract had expired in June of 1892, and union leaders were trying to resolve what appeared to be a clear-cut disagreement over wages. Frick was attempting to cut the employees' pay

> As soon as the boat carrying the Pinkertons was sighted by the pickets the alarm was sounded. The strikers were aroused from their sleep and within a few minutes the river front was covered with a crowd of coatless and hatless men armed with guns and rifles and grimly determined to prevent the landing of the Pinkertons. The latter . . . sought to intimidate the strikers by assuming a threatening attitude and aiming the muzzles of their

shining revolvers at them. . . . Then a shot was fired from the boat and one of the strikers fell to the ground mortally wounded. A howl of fury and a volley of bullets came back from the line of strikers.[42]

The battle lasted several hours, and the Pinkertons finally retreated, seeking safety in their boat. But the strikers surrounded it and eventually forced the Pinkertons to surrender. In the end, three Pinkertons and ten workers were killed, and the guards were sent packing.

Attentat

Berkman was incensed that thugs had been hired to do the bidding of what he characterized as a heartless industrialist,

---

Justifying Violence

Late in her life, Goldman spoke against violence as a means to an end (although she did not rule it out entirely). But during her early years with the anarchist movement in the United States, she passionately defended political violence as a righteous response to injustice, as in this passage from Anarchism and Other Essays.

"One must feel intensely the indignity of our social wrongs; one's very being must throb with the pain, the sorrow, the despair millions of people are daily made to endure. Indeed, unless we have become a part of humanity, we cannot even faintly understand the just indignation that accumulates in a human soul, the burning, surging passion that makes the storm inevitable.

The ignorant mass looks upon the man who makes a violent protest against our social and economic iniquities as upon a wild beast, a cruel, heartless monster, whose joy it is to destroy life and bathe in blood; or at best, as upon an irresponsible lunatic. Yet nothing is further from the truth. As a matter of fact, those who have studied the character and personality of these men, or who have come in close contact with them, are agreed that it is their super-sensitiveness to the wrong and injustice surrounding them which compels them to pay the toll of our social crimes. The most noted writers and poets, discussing the psychology of political offenders, have paid them the highest tribute. Could anyone assume that these men had advised violence, or even approved of the acts? Certainly not. Theirs was the attitude of the social student, of the man who knows that beyond every violent act there is a vital cause."

---

an oppressor of the common people. According to Goldman biographer Alice Wexler:

> The battle of July 6 electrified the three young anarchists, but in Alexander Berkman it stirred something deeper even than outrage or revolutionary fervor. To him it was the "psychologic social moment" for an *attentat*—the assassination of a powerful agent of oppression. This act, aimed at Henry Clay Frick, would "strike terror into the soul of his class" but, most important, it would dramatize the struggle of labor at Homestead. . . . In Berkman's view, murder and *attentat* were "opposite terms." He explained that "The killing of a tyrant . . . is in no way to be considered as the taking of a life. . . . To remove a tyrant is an act of liberation, the giving of life and opportunity to an oppressed people."[43]

After a fierce battle that took thirteen lives, the wounded and defeated Pinkertons surrender to the striking steelworkers.

Effects of "Prison Hells"

With firsthand knowledge of prison life, Emma Goldman was convinced that penal institutions of her day did little if anything to deter crime and that prisons should be abolished. In Anarchism and Other Essays *she writes:*

"There is not a single penal institution or reformatory in the United States where men are not tortured 'to be made good,' by means of the black-jack, the club, the strait-jacket, the water-cure, the 'humming bird' (an electrical contrivance run along the human body), the solitary . . . and starvation diet. In these institutions his will is broken, his soul degraded, his spirit subdued by the deadly monotony and routine of prison life. . . . Society might with great immunity abolish all prisons at once, than to hope for protection from these twentieth-century chambers of horrors.

Year after year the gates of prison hells return to the world an emaciated, deformed, will-less, ship-wrecked crew of humanity, with the Cain mark on their foreheads, their hopes crushed, all their natural inclinations thwarted. With nothing but hunger and inhumanity to greet them, these victims soon sink back into crime as the only possibility of existence. . . .

Well-meaning persons are now working for a new departure in the prison question,—reclamation, to restore once more to the prisoner the possibility of becoming a human being. Commendable as this is, I fear it is impossible to hope for good results. . . . Nothing short of a complete reconstruction of society will deliver mankind from the cancer of crime."

Emma Goldman supported the actions of Alexander Berkman. Even though she did not necessarily advocate violence, she believed it was justified in this case. She did what she could to prepare for the day when Berkman would go to Homestead to kill Frick. She even offered to help gain access to the office. But Berkman saw no need to sacrifice Goldman's life too.

For a week after the decision was made, Berkman experimented with bomb making by following directions in a handbook by Johann Most. As Goldman recalls:

We had a feverish week. Sasha's experiments took place when everyone was asleep. While Sasha worked, I kept watch. I lived in dread every moment for Sasha, for our friends in the flat, the children, and the rest of the tenants. What if anything should go wrong—but, then, did not the end justify the means? Our end was the sacred cause of the oppressed and exploited people. It was for them that we were going to give our lives. What if a few should have to perish?—the many would be free and could live in beauty and in comfort. Yes, the end in this case justified the means.[44]

But the means, in this case, proved quite inadequate. Whether the directions or the dynamite or Sasha's inexperience as a bomb maker was at fault, the device would not go off in tests. The would-be assassins wasted a week and forty precious dollars.

A new plan was quickly devised. Berkman would buy a pistol and go to Homestead alone. But the new plan required more money. After trying several failed avenues, Goldman begged funds from her sister Helena.

Berkman's Symbolic Act of Violence

With the twenty dollars Goldman had given him, Alexander Berkman said good-bye and rode the train to Pennsylvania. He gained entrance to Henry Frick's office by calling himself Simon Bachman, the leader of a group of strikebreakers. Berkman describes in his memoirs what happened once he was inside and saw "the look of terror" on Frick's face:

"He understands," it flashes through my mind. With a quick motion I draw the revolver. As I raise the weapon, I see Frick clutch with both hands the arm of the chair and attempt to rise. I aim at his head. "Perhaps he wears armor," I reflect. With a look of horror, he quickly averts his face, as I pull the trigger. There is a flash, and the high-ceilinged room reverberates as with the booming of a cannon. I hear a sharp piercing cry, and see Frick on his knees, his head against the arm of his chair. I feel calm and possessed, intent upon every movement of the man. He is lying head and shoulders under the large armchair, without a sound or motion. "Dead?" I wonder. I must make sure.[45]

Berkman's Arrest

Before Berkman could fire again, a man who had been meeting with Frick grabbed Berkman. In the struggle, Berkman was able to fire two more shots. Then a workman from down the hall rushed in, hit Berkman with a hammer, and knocked him to the floor.

Though he was dazed, Berkman could not mistake the voice he heard call out. It was Frick. His victim was alive. Berkman grabbed a dagger that he was carrying in his pocket and struck out repeatedly at Frick's legs, slashing him twice before being subdued and arrested.

Berkman was taken to the police station, and there, according to newspaper accounts that Goldman read in New York,

one of the detectives grew suspicious about the appearance of Berkman's face and he nearly broke the young

An illustration from an 1892 newspaper depicts Berkman's assault on industrialist Frick. Berkman received a twenty-two-year prison sentence for his attempt on Frick's life.

man's jaw trying to open his mouth. A peculiar capsule was found hidden there. When asked what it was, Berkman replied with defiant contempt: "Candy." On examination it proved to be a dynamite cartridge.[46]

Alexander Berkman had intended to commit suicide like his hero of the Hay-

market riots, Louis Lingg. Newspaper editorials harshly condemned the attempted murder, and for the first time Emma Goldman was identified in print as Berkman's friend and a dangerous anarchist.

The police tried unsuccessfully to implicate Goldman in the attack. She continued to speak out, verbally attacking the conditions Berkman had protested

Berkman in Solitary

While Berkman was in prison, Emma and Sasha stayed in touch through letters. But for a year Berkman was in solitary confinement, unable to write or read for most of that time. In July 1901, Goldman received this letter, which she includes in Living My Life.

"I have passed through a great crisis. Two of my best friends died in a frightful manner. The death of Russell, especially, affected me. He was very young, and my dearest and most devoted friend, and he died a terrible death. The doctor charged the boy with shamming, but now he says it was spinal meningitis. I cannot tell you the awful truth—it was nothing short of murder, and my poor friend rotted away by inches. When he died, they found his back one mass of bedsores. If you could read the pitiful letters he wrote, begging to see me and to be nursed by me! But the Warden wouldn't permit it. In some manner his agony seemed to communicate itself to me, and I began to experience the pains and symptoms that Russell described in his notes. . . . I suffered excruciating pain. . . . I was on the verge of suicide. I demanded to be relieved from the cell, and the Warden ordered me punished. I was put in the strait jacket. They bound my body in canvas, strapping my arms to the bed, and chained my feet to the posts. I was kept that way eight days, unable to move, rotting in my own excrement. Released prisoners called the attention of our new Inspector to my case. He refused to believe that such things were being done in the penitentiary. Reports spread that I was going blind and insane. Then the Inspector visited the hospital and had me released from the jacket.

I am in pretty bad shape, but they have put me in the general ward now, and I am glad of the chance to send you this note."

violently, and she defended him in print and in her speeches.

In the end, however, the *attentat* failed to rally popular support of the cause. The public image of anarchists as terrorists was confirmed. Berkman was sentenced to twenty-two years in prison (fifteen more than the usual sentence for the crime). Most and other anarchist leaders began to denounce acts of violence, and Goldman began to reconsider Berkman's tactics as well. The movement was now torn in half.

Chapter

4 "Red Emma"

To earn a living, Goldman returned to sewing. Meanwhile she did what she could to rally the radicals of the country behind her beloved Sasha. She wrote articles, gave speeches, and organized a group that worked to have Berkman's sentence reduced to the usual length of seven years. At one of the group's meetings, in December 1892, she met Edward Brady, a man who had just spent ten years in a European prison for publishing anarchist literature.

"He introduced me to the great classics of English and French literature," remembers Goldman. "He loved to read . . . to me. . . . His English, although with a German accent, was perfect. On one occasion I asked him where he had received his schooling. 'In prison,' he replied unhesitatingly."[47]

With Brady, Goldman finally found some joy in a relationship. Now she was finally able to experience the other side of her character, her loving, emotional side:

My little flat in the building known as the "Bohemian Republic," to which I had moved lately, became a temple of love. Often the thought would come to me that so much peace and beauty could not last; it was too wonderful, too perfect. Then I would cling to Ed

Goldman met Edward Brady shortly after his release from prison, where he had served a ten-year sentence for publishing anarchist literature.

with a trembling heart. He would hold me close and his unfailing humour would dispel my dark thoughts. "You are overworked," he would say. "The machine and your constant anxiety about Sasha are killing you."[48]

The New York Stock Exchange in a frenzy of panic selling of stocks in 1893. The event sparked a four-year economic depression in the United States.

Goldman was working ten to twelve hours a day to earn a meager living, and she spent much of her free time studying French and English and reading the classics that Brady suggested. She also kept up her organizational work on behalf of Berkman. The long hours and strain began to take their toll. Never robustly healthy, due perhaps to the harsh conditions of her childhood, Goldman became quite ill in the early months of 1893. As she reports, she "began to lose weight, and grew too weak to walk across the room. Physicians ordered immediate rest and a change of climate."[49]

Friends persuaded Goldman to leave the city and return once more to Rochester, where her sister could care for her. Once there, Helena took her to a lung specialist who diagnosed tuberculosis. The doctor ordered a special diet and rest for Goldman, and within two months she recovered sufficiently to be able to take brief walks. But the doctor still expected her to check into a sanitarium in the winter. Unforeseen events intervened, however.

Champion of the Unemployed

In 1893 a major economic downturn, spurred by panic selling of stocks on Wall

Street, caused some eight thousand businesses in the United States to fail and marked the beginning of a four-year depression that produced widespread unemployment; millions of people lost their jobs.

The unemployed were the common working men and women whom Goldman had always championed. She could not ignore their plight, and she was determined to get back into action regardless of her health, so she wired Ed Brady to let him know she was coming back to New York.

At first Brady was thrilled to see Goldman, but when she told him that she had returned to devote herself to the plight of the unemployed and the homeless, "his mood changed." She writes: "It was insanity, he urged; it would mean the loss of everything I had gained in health through my rest. . . . He would not permit it—I was his now—his, to love and protect and watch over."[50]

Goldman was torn emotionally. She wanted to hear that someone was willing to cherish and protect her, but she hated having anyone try to control her life. "His 'to hold and protect'? Did he consider me his property, a dependent or a cripple who had to be taken care of by a man?"[51] Eventually Brady backed away from his demands. He vowed to support Goldman in her new cause, hoping that her health would not deteriorate.

In the center of activity again, Emma began to thrive and her health improved quickly. She organized food drives, attended committee meetings, and spoke to the public about the issues of the unemployed. In August 1893 she helped to organize and obtain a legal permit for a mass meeting in Union Square to confront social problems and to explore government solutions. As Goldman biographer Richard Drinnon describes the meeting:

> Three to four thousand bitter, angry people, mostly unemployed, crowded into Union Square that Monday evening. They were especially aroused by the unwillingness of the state legislature to do anything for the homeless and hungry. Emma quickly sensed their mood. As often happened at such times of crisis, she spoke almost in tongues . . . seemingly possessed by a truly incandescent indignation and sympathy; on these occasions she was so inspired—so filled with an extrahuman energy—that she drew her audience part of the way up to her own heights of feeling and consciousness.[52]

After recovering from tuberculosis, Goldman returned to New York City in 1893 and resumed her activism full force, speaking out for the homeless and unemployed.

Goldman was the last scheduled to speak that day; and when she was finally introduced, she heard her "name shouted from a thousand throats." She reports in her autobiography:

As I stepped forward, I saw a dense mass before me, their pale, pinched faces upturned to me. My heart beat, my temples throbbed, and my knees shook.

"Men and women," I began amidst sudden silence, "do you not realize that the State is the worst enemy you have? It is a machine that crushes you in order to sustain the ruling class, your masters. Like naive children you put your trust in your political leaders. You make it possible for them to creep into your confidence, only to have them betray you to the first bidder. . . . Do you not see the stupidity of asking relief from Albany with immense wealth within a stone's throw from here? Fifth Avenue is laid in gold, every mansion is a citadel of wealth and power. Yet there you stand, a giant, starved and fettered, shorn of

Unemployed men wait in line at midnight to receive a handout from a New York City bakery. Goldman believed that the government was responsible for the ills of the poor.

his strength. . . . You, too, will have to learn that you have a right to share your neighbour's bread. Your neighbours—they have not only stolen your bread, but they are sapping your blood. . . . Well, then, demonstrate before the palaces of the rich; demand work. If they do not give you work, demand bread. If they deny you both, take bread. It is your sacred right!"[53]

The crowd's reaction to this speech was immediate and unmistakable. Thunderous applause followed her as she left the podium and went on to her next stop. She was in Philadelphia by the next morning, helping organize the unemployed there as well. But she was soon surprised by the headlines in that city's daily newspaper, which blasted her for inciting the crowd: "Red Emma has great swaying power; her vitriolic tongue was just what the ignorant mob needed to tear down New York."[54] The news article also noted that the police were on her trail and that a warrant had been issued for her arrest.

Goldman and the Philadelphia activists decided to hold a mass meeting on August 21. It was to be much like the New York gathering. Although she knew that New York detectives were looking for her, Goldman decided to press on with her activities. She reasoned that none of the police would be able to recognize her from photographs published in the paper. But when she arrived alone at the site of the meeting, a supporter called out that Emma was in the room, and immediately someone clamped a hand on her shoulder and told her she was under arrest.

Goldman was jailed for a time in Philadelphia and then sent back to New York City, where she was charged with inciting a riot and unlawful assemblage. Police accused her of calling for revolution and violence while speaking at Union Square. But she quickly learned that the Union Square event had little to do with the charges against her. Instead her beliefs and her ideals were on trial, as a section of the transcript including the prosecutor's questions shows:

> Q.- Do you believe in a Supreme Being, Miss Goldman?
>
> A.- No, sir, I do not.
>
> Q.- Is there any government on earth whose laws you approve?
>
> A.- No, sir, for they are all against the people.
>
> Q.- Why don't you leave this country if you don't like its laws?
>
> A.- Where shall I go? Everywhere on earth the laws are against the poor, and they tell me I cannot go to heaven, nor do I want to go there.[55]

On Blackwell's Island

Goldman was sentenced to serve a year in prison on Blackwell's Island, just off midtown Manhattan. Officials there learned of her sewing skills, so she was immediately placed in charge of the prison sewing shop, a favored assignment that created suspicion among her fellow inmates. They wondered why she received special favors. After all, this was "Red Emma," the radical firebrand, a crazy woman to be feared!

But she quickly won their support and admiration by refusing a prison matron's orders to force workers to stay at their

Prisoners march back to their cells after a day of hard labor at Blackwell's Island. Goldman fought for the rights of workers even while she served her own sentence at Blackwell's.

machines for long hours even if they were sick, very tired, or had to use the bathroom. As always she was fighting for the rights of the common worker. But after two months in the shop she suffered an attack of rheumatism and was confined to the hospital. There she helped other patients who were in worse health than she was. A hospital doctor was impressed with Goldman's concern for others and began to train her in nursing techniques. Within a month she was in charge of the clinic.

During her prison term Goldman continued to improve her nursing abilities, and she studied and read English-language books constantly. After ten months she became fluent in English and she had sufficient skills to be employed as a nurse. But she had not lost the revolutionary fire that had been fanned on her arrival in New York City five years earlier. On the contrary, when she was released from prison on August 17, 1894, she was eager to speak to the twenty-eight hundred supporters who were on hand at the Thalia Theater to greet her. According to one biographer, Emma addressed the crowd in German and in English:

Friends and comrades, I have come back to you after having served ten months in prison for talking. If the representatives of your Government intend to prosecute women for talking, they will have to begin with their mothers, wives, sisters, and sweethearts, for they will never stop women from talking (cheers). But it was not Emma Goldman who was prosecuted. It was the thoughts of Emma Goldman, the principles of Anarchy, that

A Prison Friend

Though Goldman often proclaimed that she followed no religion and was an atheist, she enjoyed the friendship of a young priest while serving her first prison term on Blackwell's Island. Goldman describes her respect for the priest in her autobiography, Living My Life.

"At first I felt antagonistic to him. I thought he was like the rest of the religious busybodies, but I soon found that he wanted to talk only about books. He had studied in Cologne and had read much. He knew I had many books and he asked me to exchange some of them with him. I was amazed and wondered what kind of books he would bring me, expecting the New Testament or the Catechism. But he came with works of poetry and music. He had free access to the prison at any time, and often he would come to the ward at nine in the evening and remain till after midnight. We would discuss his favourite composers—Bach, Beethoven, and Brahms—and compare our views on poetry and social ideas. He presented me with an English-Latin dictionary as a gift, inscribed: 'With the highest respect, to Emma Goldman.'

On one occasion I asked him why he never gave me the Bible. 'Because no one can understand or love it if he is forced to read it,' he replied. That appealed to me and I asked him for it. Its simplicity of language and legendry fascinated me. There was no make-believe about my young friend. He was devout, entirely consecrated. He observed every fast and he would lose himself in prayer for hours. Once he asked me to help him decorate the chapel. When I came down, I found the frail, emaciated figure in silent prayer, oblivious of his surroundings. My own ideal, my faith, was at the opposite pole from his, but I knew he was as ardently sincere as I. Our fervour was our meeting-ground."

were prosecuted; the views held by thousands of brave men and women who have died and are ready to die. . . . It was the right of free speech that was prosecuted in the Court of General Sessions, and not little Emma Goldman.[56]

In Transition

The training that Goldman had received while in prison led to work as a practical nurse with the doctor who had befriended her at Blackwell's. Although the work was gratifying, she wanted to advance in the profession and knew that further study was necessary. So at Ed Brady's urging, she traveled to Europe in 1895 to study medicine.

Goldman also continued her work as a political activist in Europe, attending lectures and speaking out occasionally. But she kept a very low profile. Her goal at the time was mastery in the healing arts, and she enrolled in classes in Vienna, where she was able to hear many eminent lecturers of the day, among them the young Sigmund Freud.

At the end of the term Goldman received certificates in nursing and midwifery and in the fall of 1896 returned to New York. There she worked as a midwife, helping newly arrived, poor, European immigrants deliver their babies.

Unfortunately Goldman's own health was not good. She had recurring pains in her legs that would cause her to fall to the floor immobilized for minutes at a time, a condition she suffered throughout her life. But poor health seldom prevented her from moving ahead toward whatever objective she set for herself.

A Break with Ed Brady

Conflict between Goldman and Ed Brady had simmered for a long time. Emma was concerned that Ed did not understand her need to lead an independent life. She was herself in a quandary about what her relationship with a man should be. She loved the attention but hated the controls that Ed took for granted: a man should take care of a woman. Period. So she would go to her meetings at night, but become tense if they ran late because Ed

While studying medicine in Europe, Goldman attended a lecture by the well-known psychologist Sigmund Freud.

Overcoming Bitterness

Goldman's "beloved sister Helena" had tried over the years to persuade her to reconcile with her father, but the relationship between father and daughter had remained mutually hostile. Eventually, though, after an absence of five years, Goldman paid a short visit to her sick father and began to understand why Abraham had been so harsh most of his life. As Goldman writes in Living My Life:

"On that visit I found Father physically broken, a mere shadow of his former strong and energetic self. . . . Ten hours' work in the shop . . . were destructive to his weakened and nervous state of health, aggravated by the taunts and indignities he had to endure. He was the only Jew, a man of nearly fifty, a foreigner not familiar with the language of the country. Most of the youngsters who worked with him were of foreign parents, but they had acquired the worst American traits. . . . They were crude, coarse, and heartless. . . . Repeatedly they had so molested and harassed him as to cause him to faint. He would be brought home, only to compel himself to go back the next day. He could not afford to lose the job that paid him ten dollars a week.

The sight of Father so ill and worn softened the last vestige of my animosity towards him. I began to regard him as one of the mass of the exploited and enslaved for whom I was living and working.

Helena had always argued that Father's violence in his youth had been due to his exceptional energy, which found no adequate outlet in such a small place as Popelan. He had been ambitious for himself and his family. . . . The failure of his life, the lack of opportunity to put his abilities to good use, had embittered him and made him ill-natured and hard towards his own."

might be upset. She loved him, but she saw the break coming. "More and more I had become convinced that my life would never know harmony in love for very long, that strife and not peace would be my lot."[57]

When Goldman was asked to tour the country again as a speaker, even Ed knew that she should pursue the opportunity. A change of scene and a break from her long working hours would do her good and perhaps improve her health.

On the Road Again

As Goldman prepared for her lectures, events in Spain began to determine her approach. A modern Inquisition was taking place in that country. Spain's prime minister, Canovas del Castillo, ordered mass arrests of trade unionists and anarchists, holding them in prison for days without food or water and torturing them to obtain false confessions. The American press was not reporting the atrocities, so Goldman and her friends decided to speak out about the conditions in Spain, advertising her lecture on the subject.

Immediately newspaper editorials "began to urge the authorities to stop 'Red Emma,' that term having stuck to me since the Union Square meeting," Emma writes in her autobiography. "On the night of our gathering the police appeared in full force, crowding even the platform so that the speakers could hardly make a gesture without touching an officer."[58]

As usual, Goldman's speech raised the emotional level of the crowd to fever pitch. A voice cried out to her from the audience asking if she thought a representative of the Spanish government in Washington or New York should be killed in revenge for conditions she had described. Sensing that this was a trap to get her to advocate murder and incite a riot, she responded, "No, I do not think any one of the Spanish representatives in America is important enough to be killed, but if I were in Spain now, I should kill Canovas del Castillo."[59]

Spanish Prime Minister Assassinated

Several weeks later news arrived from Spain that an anarchist named Angiolillo had shot and killed the prime minister.

Soon everyone was after Goldman for a comment.

> Reporters pestered me day and night for interviews. Did I know the man? had I been in correspondence with him? had I suggested to him that Canovas be killed? I had to disappoint them. I did not know Angiolillo and had never corresponded with him. All I knew was that he had acted while the rest of us had only talked about the fearful outrages.[60]

Goldman's comments kept her in the public eye. Statements from a fiery woman could sell a lot of newspapers, and Goldman could always be counted on to say something mainstream America would find outrageous. The notoriety followed her on tour, and when she appeared in Providence, Rhode Island, the police were on the alert. As Goldman explains:

> I had spoken in Providence a number of times without the least trouble. Rhode Island was still one of the few States to maintain the old tradition of unabridged freedom of speech. Two of our open-air gatherings, attended by thousands went off well. But the police had evidently decided to suppress our last meeting. . . . My good comrade John H. Cook, a very active worker, opened the meeting, and I began to speak. Just then a policeman came running towards us, shouting: "Stop your jabbering! Stop it this minute or I'll pull you off the box!" I went on talking. Someone called out: "Don't mind the bully—go right on!" The policeman came up, puffing heavily. When he got his breath he snarled, "Say, you, are you deaf? Didn't I tell

you to stop? What d'you mean not obeying the law?" "Are you the law?" I retorted; "I thought it is your duty to maintain the law, not to break it. Don't you know the law in this State gives me the right of free speech?" "The hell it does," he replied, "I'm the law."[61]

Goldman was knocked from the box and set upon by a gang of club-swinging policemen. The officer who had ordered her to stop talking grabbed her and yelled to his partners: "Drive those damn anarchists back so I can get this woman. She's under arrest." Once at the police station, Goldman demanded to know why she had been arrested and why her rights had been violated. According to Goldman, the desk sergeant replied: "'Because you're Emma Goldman. . . . Anarchists have no rights in this community, see?' He ordered me locked up for the night."[62]

Released from jail the next day, Goldman continued her extensive tour of the United States, speaking to crowds large and small about her ideas for a just society. Her interest in medicine had not faded, however, and in 1899 two wealthy friends, Herman Miller and Carl Stone, provided the funds for her to go to Europe and begin studies to become a doctor.

A Goal Deferred

While in London, Goldman met a Czech revolutionist named Hippolyte Havel. The two became lovers, and when Goldman left for Paris to begin classes, Havel went with her. But instead of going to classes they attended secret meetings with other radicals and anarchists.

Upon Goldman's arrival in Europe she met Czech revolutionist Hippolyte Havel.

Miller and Stone, Goldman's benefactors, were angered by her actions and they demanded she return to her studies. As Stone wrote: "I am interested only in E.G. the woman—her ideas have absolutely no meaning whatever to me. Please choose." But Goldman would not be controlled, even by those who would pay to help her achieve her career dream. She wrote in response: "E.G. the woman and her ideas are inseparable. She does not exist for the amusement of upstarts, nor will she permit anybody to dictate to her. Keep your money."[63]

Goldman put her goal of becoming a doctor aside; more valuable to her were discussions with the leading anarchists of Europe, which led her to establish the political goals that would direct her activities for many years to come. According to biographer Alice Wexler, Goldman

> did not attempt to organize her ideas in a systematic way, but developed them in her lectures, pamphlets, in articles published in both the anarchist and commercial press, and even in interviews. . . . Goldman's political thought, as it emerged in the late nineties, [was a blend of] communist anarchism with . . . individualism . . . and a strong emphasis on women's emancipation and sexual freedom. . . . Less interested in theory than in practice, she used these ideas to criticize contemporary society and to propose change.[64]

With Havel, Goldman returned to New York on December 7, 1900. Armed with her ideas, the thirty-one-year-old Goldman set off once more throughout the United States, speaking and writing about the need to throw off government in all of its forms. As she argues in a pamphlet written about this time, the state was not a natural outgrowth of human necessity:

> There was a time when the state was unknown. In his natural condition man existed without any State or organized government. People lived as families in small communities; they tilled the soil and practiced the arts and crafts. The individual, and later the family, was the unit of social life where each was free and the equal of his neighbor. Human society then was not a State but an association; a voluntary association for mutual protection and benefit. . . . Political government and the State were a much later development, growing out of the desire of the stronger to take advantage of the weaker, of the few against the many.[65]

Chapter

5 The Assassination of President McKinley

In 1901 Goldman began a new speaking and organizing tour that took her to major cities across the country. On September 6, she was standing on a corner in St. Louis, Missouri, waiting for a streetcar to arrive when she was startled by the cry of a newsboy hawking his paper: "'Extra! Extra! President McKinley shot!' I bought a paper, but the car was so jammed that it was impossible to read. Around me people

A gunman rushes toward President McKinley and shoots him at close range. Almost immediately, authorities tried to implicate Goldman in the attack.

were talking about the shooting of the President."[66]

At the home of friends where she was staying, she learned that McKinley had been shot while he was in a receiving line at the Pan-American Exposition in Buffalo, New York. The young gunman was caught immediately.

Partly in jest a friend noted that Goldman was lucky she was not in Buffalo because the newspapers would connect her with the attack on the president. But Goldman couldn't believe such a thing could occur, even if reporters did make farfetched claims where radicals, especially Goldman, were concerned.

The next morning she found that her friend's prediction was right on the mark. In a stationery store Goldman happened to glance at the headline of a newspaper lying on a nearby desk: "Assassin Of President McKinley An Anarchist. Confesses To Having Been Incited By Emma Goldman. Woman Anarchist Wanted."[67] Shocked but trying to stay calm, she quickly finished her business in the store and left.

Goldman immediately bought several newspapers, which were filled with stories that assumed McKinley had been killed outright. But a few hours later news bulletins stated that the president was rallying after surgery to remove a bullet from his abdomen. Doctors, however, were concerned about the seriousness of the president's injuries and the danger of infection.

The Czolgosz Connection

When the first reports about the assault on the president appeared in the newspa-

McKinley assassin Leon Czolgosz (pictured) had met Goldman briefly a few weeks before his attack on the president.

pers, they were accompanied by a photograph of the attacker. Goldman was astonished to see a face she recognized. The attacker was identified in the newspaper as Leon Czolgosz, but Goldman had been introduced to him when he was using another name. As she recalls, she met him on the day she was packing her belongings and preparing to leave the home of two Chicago friends, Abraham and Mary Isaak, publishers of a popular anarchist newspaper:

Mary Isaak came in to tell me that a young man, who gave his name as Nieman, was urgently asking to see me. I knew nobody by that name and I was in a hurry, about to leave for the station. Rather impatiently I requested

Mary to inform the caller that I had no time at the moment, but that he could talk to me on the way to the station.[68]

Goldman soon realized that she had briefly talked with this man—known as Nieman—at a meeting in Cleveland some weeks before. "Nieman told me that he had belonged to a Socialist local in Cleveland, that he had found its members dull, lacking in vision and enthusiasm. He could not bear to be with them and he had left Cleveland and was now working in Chicago and eager to get in touch with anarchists."[69] When they arrived at the station, Goldman turned the young man over to Hippolyte Havel, who had settled in the area, and she asked her friend to introduce Nieman to his comrades.

With that Goldman boarded the train for her next destination. She had no further contact with the man identified as Leon Czolgosz.

The Arrest

For a few days President McKinley showed signs of improvement, but gangrene was spreading throughout his body; there were no drugs at that time to counteract the infection and decay. As McKinley's condition worsened, police in several major cities searched for Goldman, questioning her family and friends. In Chicago, police raided the Isaaks' home. Because Goldman had stayed with the Isaaks a few months earlier, Chicago police arrested the couple and several visitors. News accounts stated that all would be jailed until Emma Goldman was found. Two hundred detectives had been assigned to track her down.

Goldman decided to return to Chicago so that her friends would be released from jail. After all, the Isaaks were not guilty of anything other than knowing the infamous Red Emma and sympathizing with her views.

Risking arrest was truly an act of courage on Goldman's part. Even though she was not connected to the president's assailant in any way, apart from having spoken to him, she was a hated woman. She spoke her mind and was willing to live up to her radical ideals, but such actions seemed to threaten most of the "normal" society at the turn of the century. In fact, Emma Goldman's name had become "synonymous with everything vile and criminal," according to biographer Alice Wexler. And one newspaper in San Francisco had stated what many Americans thought about Emma Goldman when they labeled her "'a despicable creature,' a 'snake,' 'unfit to live in a civilized country.' Not a few people would have applauded the proposal that she 'be hanged by the neck until dead and considerably longer.'"[70]

Many of Emma's friends counseled her to stay away from Chicago. "They argued with me for hours," she recalls, "but they failed to change my decision. I told them jokingly that they had better give me a good send-off, as we probably should never again have an opportunity for a jolly evening together." A few hours later she was resting in her berth on the sleeping car headed for Chicago. "The car was agog with the Buffalo tragedy, Czolgosz and Emma Goldman. 'A beast, a bloodthirsty monster!' I heard someone say; 'she should have been locked up long ago.' 'Locked up nothing!' another retorted; 'she should be strung up to the first lamp-post.'"[71]

Goldman stayed hidden for a few days in Chicago, but police soon found and arrested her. She was immediately subjected to the "third degree"—intensive questioning that lasted several days. But there was no way for the Chicago police to implicate her in the attack on the president. Eventually the chief of police questioned her personally. He walked away from Emma's cell convinced that she was telling the truth. "Unless you're a very clever actress, you are certainly innocent, and I am going to do my part to help you out," he told Emma.[72]

While Emma was jailed, a reporter from the *New York Times* interviewed her, and she tried to explain her feelings about the situation:

> Leon Czolgosz, I am convinced, planned the deed unaided and entirely alone. There is no Anarchist ring which would help him. There may be Anarchists who would murder, but there are also men in every walk of life who sometimes feel the impulse to kill. I do not know surely, but I think

Czolgosz was one of those downtrodden men who see all the misery which the rich inflict upon the poor, who think of it, who brood over it, and then, in despair, resolve to strike a blow, as they think, for the good of their fellow-men. But that is not Anarchy. Czolgosz . . . may have been inspired by me, but if he was, he took the wrong way of showing it.[73]

No Relief

Regardless of the fact that the Chicago authorities had no leads to support a conspiracy and no evidence that Emma Goldman was involved in Czolgosz's act, the prosecutor in Buffalo asked that she be returned to his jurisdiction. Eventually his request was thrown out because no hard evidence could be produced to implicate Goldman. But in an attempt to piece together a conspiracy between the anarchists Goldman and Czolgosz, the police grilled Czolgosz at length. During one

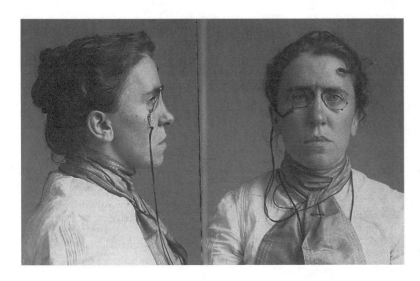

Goldman was arrested and jailed for her suspected involvement in the assassination of President McKinley. She was released after the police were unable to find any solid evidence against her.

A Long-Lasting Reputation

Years after the death of President McKinley, author Margaret Leech, who wrote about his life, still blamed Emma Goldman for instigating his assassination and suggested a conspiracy, even though records clearly show otherwise. In Leech's 1959 book In the Days of McKinley *she writes:*

"The news of the attack on the President spread horror throughout the nation. The bare statement, sent over the AP wires only two or three minutes after Czolgosz fired, had reached the cities in time to make the last editions. . . .

The newspapers . . . had reported that the President's assailant was an anarchist, who boasted that he had done his duty. The excited emotions of the country found vent in demanding reprisals against all anarchists everywhere. It was not for an instant credited that Czolgosz had acted alone. The deed had the menace and the insolence of conspiracy. A hunt for his accomplices was pressed in Cleveland, Chicago, Detroit, and other industrial centers. Hundreds of anarchist sympathizers were questioned, and some were arrested and detained. Second only to Czolgosz in popular odium was Emma Goldman, whom he had spoken of with admiration to the police. She was generally supposed to have instigated his crime, and there was high satisfaction when she was tracked down and arrested in Chicago."

interrogation held the night of the shooting, he specifically denied that Goldman was involved in any manner, as this portion of the transcript shows:

Q.-Have you ever taken any obligation or sworn any oath to kill anybody; you have haven't you; look up and speak; haven't you done that?

A.-No sir.

Q.-Who was the last one you heard talk [against rulers]?

A.-Emma Goldman.

Q.-You heard her say it would be a good thing if all these rulers were wiped off the face of the earth?

A.-She didn't say that.

Q.-What did she say? What did she say about the president?

A.-She says—she didn't mention no presidents at all; she mentioned the government.

Q.-What did she say about it?

A.-She said she didn't believe in it.

The front page of a 1901 issue of the New York World *calls Goldman a "wrinkled, ugly, Russian woman who owns no God" and connects her to President McKinley's murder.*

Q.-And that all those who supported the government ought to be destroyed; did she believe in that?

A.-She didn't say they ought to be destroyed.

Q.-You wanted to help her in her work, and thought this was the best way to do it; was that your idea; or if you have any other idea, tell us what it was?

A.-She didn't tell me to do it. [74]

President McKinley died just a week after being shot, on September 14, and the nation seemed to erupt in sorrow and anger. Even though Czolgosz, the confessed assassin, was in custody, that did little to appease the general ugly mood.

Release and Depression

When police released Emma Goldman after fifteen days in jail and the loss of a tooth caused by the blow from a policeman's fist, there was considerable public outcry. People made Goldman the target of their hate and fear. Parents warned their children that if they didn't behave they would end up "like Emma Goldman" or that if they weren't good "Red Emma would get them." Seven-year-old Margaret Leech (who later wrote extensively about McKinley) was living in a New York hotel at the time, and wrote a poem reflecting the general sentiment of the day:

> I am oh so sorry
> That our President is dead,
> And everybody's sorry
> so my father said; And the horrid man who killed him
> Is a-sitting in his cell
> And I'm glad that Emma Goldman
> Doesn't board at this hotel. [75]

The McKinley assassination prompted the first concerted effort to halt Goldman's activities, an effort she had long expected. What she did not foresee was the way some "friends" would abandon the cause at the first sign of trouble. The Isaaks and other radical publishers tried to distance themselves from the assassination and the assassin, calling him a spy, which was untrue. Goldman, always true to her ideals, refused to compromise and spoke out in support of young Czolgosz for acting on his beliefs. For this, many in the radical community turned against her.

When Leon Czolgosz was executed on October 29, 1901, however, Goldman did begin to back away from her public life.

Czolgosz sits strapped to an electric chair in the final moments before his execution.

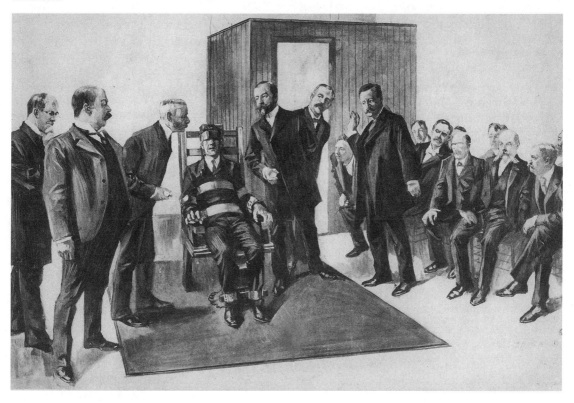

McKinley and the Anarchists

Because many believed Goldman played a role in McKinley's death, she was harassed for years afterward, and her family became targets for attack, as biographer Richard Drinnon explains in Rebel in Paradise:

"In Rochester the Goldman family was submitted to police questioning and popular persecution. Emma's teenage niece, Stella Cominsky, was mercilessly interrogated for two days, but she stoutly maintained that her Tante [Aunt] Emma was innocent. Her other nephews and nieces had innumerable jeers to bear at school about their aunt who was a "murderess." But her father suffered most. Abraham Goldman lost many of his customers in his little furniture store, was ostracized by his neighbors, and was even excommunicated from his synagogue."

Being "Red Emma" was wearing her down. It was even hard to find a place to live, as no landlord wanted to take a chance with her. She became more and more withdrawn.

It was bitter hard to face life anew. In the stress of the past several weeks I had forgotten that I should again have to take up the struggle for existence. It was doubly imperative; I needed forgetfulness. Our movement had lost its appeal to me; many of its adherents filled me with loathing. They had been flaunting anarchism like a red cloth before a bull, but they ran to cover at his first charge. I could no longer work with them. Still more harrowing was the gnawing doubt of the values I had so fervently believed in. No, I could not continue in the movement. I must first take stock of my own self.[76]

Goldman worked a midnight shift taking care of immigrants at a hospital, then returned to her flat to sleep the daylight hours away. It was a way of avoiding a world that now proved too difficult to confront.

6 From "Red Emma" to *Mother Earth*

The qualities that I had most admired in the heroes of the past, and also in Czolgosz, the strength to stand and die alone, had been lacking in me. Perhaps one needs more courage to live than to die. Dying is of a moment, but the claims of life are endless—a thousand small and petty things which tax one's strength and leave one too spent to meet the testing hour.[77]

This is how Goldman analyzed the months of depression she experienced in 1901 and 1902. But frequent news of the hazardous working conditions in U.S. mines, such as poisonous gases and cave-ins that killed many miners, began to fuel her activist impulses. She also read horror stories about Russian peasants and laborers who were organizing against the czarist government and were often brutally beaten—sometimes flogged to death—and imprisoned for long terms. Unable to tolerate these injustices and brutalities, she was drawn back into the world she knew so well. "I emerged from my tortuous

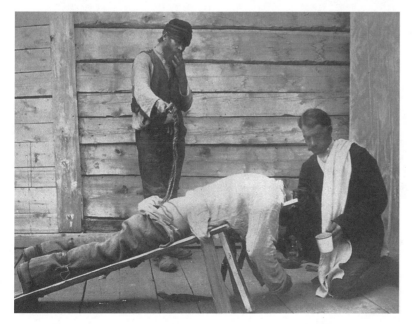

An early-twentieth-century photo reveals the brutal torture of a Russian worker who spoke against his czarist government. Goldman emerged from her lengthy depression determined to help such laborers who were persecuted for voicing their opinions.

introspection as from a long illness, not yet in possession of my former vigor, but with a determination to try once more to steel my will to meet the exigencies of life, whatever they might be," she writes. [78]

As if to prove to herself that she was yet the Emma Goldman of old, she threw herself into a new lecture tour, designed to raise money to help U.S. miners who were striking for better working conditions. Goldman also wanted to aid Russian peasants and workers.

While on tour, Goldman had to deal with constant police harassment wherever she was scheduled to speak. As she reports:

> My tour was trying and strenuous, made more so by the necessity of speaking surrounded by watch-dogs ready to spring on me at any moment, as well as by being compelled to change halls at a moment's notice. But I welcomed the difficulties. They helped to rekindle my fighting spirit and to convince me that those in power never learn to what extent persecution is the leaven of [heightens] revolutionary zeal.[79]

The Anarchist Exclusion Act

In 1903 the U.S. government took the kind of action that Goldman had long been warning people about in her speeches. Congress passed a bill legalizing the exclusion and deportation of alien anarchists—those who were not U.S. citizens—from the United States. This meant that any alien who had ever advocated a form of social organization other than a

In 1903 Goldman embarked on a lengthy speaking tour of the United States. Goldman used the tour, which she called "trying and strenuous," to fight for workers' rights.

government based on law could be barred from entry. Likewise, any resident alien branded an anarchist was subject to deportation. Goldman was exempt under the law because of her marriage to a naturalized citizen, Kershner. But she decided to fight loudly and adamantly against the act.

American libertarian activists began to mobilize too. Libertarians believed in the primacy of individual liberty much as anarchists did, and they shared Goldman's view that society should be based on personal freedom and voluntary shared ownership of property. Libertarians had always been staunch defenders of the right of free speech as well, but Goldman noted their surge of activism with some sarcasm:

Too late did the lukewarm liberals [Libertarians] realize the peril of this law to advanced thought. Had they opposed in a concerted manner the activities of the reactionary element, the statute might not have been passed. The immediate result of this new assault on American liberties, however, was a very decided change of attitude towards anarchists. I myself now ceased to be considered anathema [a detested person]; on the contrary, the very people who had been hostile to me began to seek me out.[80]

Goldman was invited to speak to various libertarian or liberal organizations. These groups were eager to lend her their support now that anarchists were considered "oppressed" because of their beliefs. Prior to this time Goldman's audiences were mostly working-class German and Russian immigrants. Now she had the opportunity "to reach the native intelligentsia, to enlighten it as to what anarchism really means."[81] In other words, she was finally able to address her ideas to the people who had the most power in the anarchist movement: those born in the United States.

The Free Speech League

With their support, Goldman, working under the name E. G. Smith, organized a branch of the Free Speech League, one of several societies formed at the time to defend the right of free speech. Among its members were some of the most prominent American liberal thinkers and activists of the day. Their first cause was to fight the deportation of a British anarchist, John Turner, who had come to the United States at the invitation of Goldman and some of her friends for a lecture tour.

A prominent labor leader in his own country, Turner was a high-profile figure. The U.S. government decided to make him its first example under the Anarchist Exclusion Act of 1903, and he was arrested as he took the stage in New York City to deliver his first speech. A local paper noted that "when the anarchist speaker was put under arrest, his audience was inclined to rescue him by force, and a riot threatened, but Emma Goldman, the Anarchist leader, sprang to the platform and succeeded in controlling her followers."[82]

Goldman's Free Speech League fought to prevent the deportation of John Turner, a British anarchist who was one of the first to fall under the Anarchist Exclusion Act of 1903.

Peter Kropotkin

Goldman frequently organized speaking tours in the United States for such other well-known anarchists as Peter Kropotkin, who fought injustices against peasants, workers, and soldiers in Russia. In Kill the Tsar! Youth and Terrorism in Old Russia, *author K.C. Tessendor includes these words from Kropotkin:*

"Don't let anyone tell us that we—but a small band—are too weak to attain unto the magnificent end at which we aim. Count and see how many there are who suffer this injustice. We peasants who work for others, and who mumble the straw while our master eats the wheat, we by ourselves are millions of men. We workers who weave silks and velvet in order that we may be clothed in rags, we, too, are a great multitude; and when the clang of the factories permits us a moment's repose, we overflow the streets and squares like the sea in a spring tide. We soldiers who are driven along to the word of command, or by blows, we who receive the bullets for which our officers get crosses and pensions, we, too, poor fools who have hitherto known no better than to shoot our brothers, why we have only to make a right about-face towards those plumed and decorated personages who are so good as to command us, to see a ghastly pallor overspread their faces.

Ay, all of us together, we who suffer and are insulted daily, we are a multitude whom no man can number, we are the ocean that can embrace and swallow up all else. When we have but the will to do it, that very moment will justice be done: that very instant the tyrants of the earth shall bite the dust."

Russian anarchist Peter Kropotkin gave a voice to the peasants, workers, and soldiers in Russia who faced innumerable injustices.

The Free Speech League hired one of the most respected lawyers of the day, Clarence Darrow, and his partner, Edgar Lee Masters, to defend Turner before the U.S. Supreme Court. Goldman independently raised $1,600 for the defense fund and conducted a publicity campaign designed to raise public awareness of the issues involved. However, as Goldman reports, "When the decision was finally handed down it proved to be just what we had expected. It upheld the constitutionality of the anti-anarchist law and sustained the order for Turner's deportation."[83] Nevertheless the case prompted activists across the United States to organize free speech societies, which succeeded in uniting many citizens concerned about exercising their free speech rights.

A Fortunate Twist of Fate

Between 1903 and 1906 Goldman continued speaking and organizing to defend the right of free speech and to advance such causes as individual liberty, women's rights, free love (the belief that each individual should be free to determine her or his own sexual behavior), and fair pay and better working conditions for laborers. She also concentrated on the problems of her native Russia, which in 1905 was undergoing the throes of a revolution against the czar.

Throughout this time she worked long hours as a private nurse, and the anxiety of that job began to take its toll. She writes that "Every rise in the temperature of my charges used to alarm me, and a death would upset me for weeks."[84] She needed

Lawyer Clarence Darrow (pictured) tried unsuccessfully to defend Turner at his U.S. Supreme Court deportation trial.

less stressful work if she was to continue her "platform activities," as she called her speaking engagements.

A friend recommended that Goldman set up shop as a masseuse, giving facial and scalp massages. After borrowing $300 and renting a shop with plenty of sunlight and a fine view of the East River on Broadway and Seventeenth Street, she was in business.

Most of Goldman's clientele consisted of Russian friends who would come in to get a massage and discuss current issues. Because she was among friends, Goldman could work under her real name, which she found impossible to do when she was

Proudhon's Influence

Goldman and other anarchists read the works of such revolutionaries as Frenchman Pierre-Joseph Proudhon, known as the true father of anarchism and the first to call himself an anarchist. Biographer Alix Shulman includes one of Proudhon's dramatic statements in To the Barricades: The Anarchist Life of Emma Goldman.

"To be governed is to be watched over, inspected, spied on, directed, legislated at, regulated, docketed, indoctrinated, preached at, controlled, assessed, weighed, censored, ordered about, by men who have neither the right nor the virtue. To be governed means . . . to be, on the pretext of the general interest, taxed, drilled, held to ransom, exploited, monopolized, extorted, squeezed, hoaxed, robbed; then at the least resistance, at the first word of complaint, to be repressed, fined, abused, annoyed, followed, bullied, beaten, disarmed, garroted, imprisoned, machine-gunned, judged, condemned, deported, flayed, sold, betrayed, and finally mocked, ridiculed, insulted, dishonored. That's government, that's its justice, that's its morality!"

Frenchman Pierre-Joseph Proudhon, known as the father of anarchism, had a profound influence on Goldman.

a nurse. People were leery of being cared for by the infamous Miss Goldman, so she resorted to the pseudonym E. G. Smith to gain employment. The new business relieved a great deal of stress in her life and allowed her to earn some money. Indirectly it also led to one of her most fortunate contacts.

In the late summer of 1905 Goldman was forced to suspend her business temporarily because her clients had all left the city for cooler spots. She and a few women friends decided that they might as well do the same. So they found a place on Hunter Island in Pelham Bay, near New York City, pitched a tent, and planned a relaxing stay along the shore.

News soon reached them that the great Russian actor Pavel Orleneff and his acting company had been booted from their New York apartments for failing to pay rent. The troupe had been traveling America presenting plays to protest the wave of pogroms—persecutions—that was sweeping Russia. Goldman had attended all of the New York performances and felt that "nothing like its ensemble acting had ever been seen on the American stage before. It was therefore a shock to learn that Orleneff's troupe, who had given us so much, should find themselves stranded, without friends or funds. We might pitch a tent for Orleneff on our island, I thought."[85] And that is exactly what happened. Within a week the whole troupe had arrived and set up camp.

Goldman and Orleneff became close friends, and the actor eventually persuaded her to become his interpreter, agent, and manager. Soon she was calling on friends and benefactors in many parts of the country to arrange performances, to which she traveled the following winter under her assumed name. Many a patron of the performances was startled to learn later that the company's poised and elegant road manager was America's most famous anarchist.

Mother Earth Is Born

The friendship between Goldman and the actor grew. Orleneff asked her once what she would like to do most if she had money, and she replied that her greatest desire was "to publish a magazine that would combine my social ideals with the young strivings in the various art forms in America." Orleneff then "offered to give a special performance for the purpose."[86]

A date was set and a hall was rented, with the hope that the troupe would earn at least $2,000 to invest in Goldman's magazine. But on the night of the performance a torrential rain kept most of the crowd away, and the proceeds amounted to only $250—not much to start a magazine.

Goldman was undeterred. On March 1, 1906, the first sixty-four-page issue of her magazine, *Mother Earth*, appeared. It contained articles by some of the most prominent libertarian and anarchist thinkers, who explored subjects such as the fundamentals of anarchism and the need for labor parties; and Goldman's own contribution, "The Tragedy of Woman's Emancipation." That "tragedy," she explained, was the fact that women were not truly equal to men in status or income and did not have the same freedoms men had in society. Women were, in her words, "slaves to their husbands and children." As she wrote in her conclusion:

The movement for woman's emancipation has so far made but the first step in that direction. . . . The right to vote, or equal civil rights, may be good demands, but true emancipation begins neither at the polls nor in the courts. It begins in woman's soul. . . . It is, therefore, far more important for her to . . . cut loose from the weight of prejudices, traditions, and customs. The demand for equal rights in every vocation of life is just and fair; but, after all, the most vital right is the right to love and be loved. . . . Complete and true emancipation . . . will have to do away with the ridiculous notion that to be loved . . . is synonymous with being slave or subordinate. It will have to do away with the absurd notion of the dualism of the sexes, or that man and woman represent two antagonistic worlds.[87]

Mother Earth published numerous essays and reports from anarchists in the United States and in Europe: articles about labor unions and strikes, legal battles for free speech, campaigns for birth control, and many other subjects relating to and promoting individual liberty.

Though she left most of the editing and production work to others, Goldman controlled its content, publishing her speeches on the emerging feminist movement and her well-developed opinions regarding individual freedom in all aspects of life. She also wanted the magazine to demonstrate the social value of modern literature, so she published excerpts from plays, essays, and poems, including the work of the nineteenth-century American poet Walt Whitman and essayists/poets Henry David Thoreau and Ralph Waldo Emerson, all of whom expressed strong beliefs in individual liberty and opposition to authority. In fact, Thoreau's statement, "That government is best that governs not at all," could have served as an anarchist motto.

Goldman also used the magazine to question the tactics and policies of the government. As such it was an important vehicle for her to establish her legitimacy as a leader of the political Left—people who advocated the reform or overthrow of the existing social order. *Mother Earth* was well received in radical circles and found loyal readers among some college students and artists.

Determined to have her views heard, Goldman published Mother Earth, *a magazine devoted to social ideals and the arts.*

Goldman included the writings of poet/essayist Ralph Waldo Emerson in her magazine Mother Earth.

In May 1906, however, Goldman was distracted by an event of great personal significance. Alexander Berkman, with whom she had been corresponding and visiting occasionally over the long years, was about to be released from the Pennsylvania penitentiary. After fourteen years, part of it spent in solitary confinement, her great love, Sasha, was about to be freed.

Berkman's Return

On the day that Sasha was released—May 18, 1906—Emma went with friends to the Detroit train station to meet him. She was standing on the platform lost in thought when someone began calling that the train had arrived. Two of her friends ran ahead, but Goldman recalls that she

> remained riveted to the ground, clutching at the post, my heart throbbing violently.

> My friends returned, a stranger walking between them, with swaying step. . . . The strange-looking man—was that Sasha, I wondered. His face deathly white, eyes covered with large, ungainly glasses; his hat too big for him, too deep over his head—he looked pathetic, forlorn.[88]

As Emma and Sasha met once more after so long a time, neither could speak. Emma simply handed him the roses she had brought and kissed him.

Chapter

7 Government Victories

Alexander Berkman found it very difficult to adjust to life outside a cell. He was withdrawn, sullen, and emotionally cold. Imprisonment had taken a great toll on the enthusiastic young rebel Goldman had met the first day of her arrival in New York City. For his part, Berkman found Goldman changed, too. Just after his release, he wrote in his *Prison Memoirs*:

My companion of the days that thrilled with the approach of the Social Revolution, has become a woman of the world. Her mind has matured, but her wider interests antagonize my old revolutionary traditions. . . . I feel an instinctive disapproval of many things. . . . Her friends and admirers crowd her home, and turn it into a

After his release from prison, Berkman began a lecture tour in support of Goldman's causes. Here, Berkman speaks to New York City laborers in 1908.

Goldman speaks at a 1916 rally in New York City.

sort of a salon. They talk art and literature; discuss science and philosophy over the disharmony of life. . . . I resent the situation, the more I become conscious of the chasm between the Girl and myself. It seems unbridgeable; we cannot recover the intimate note of our former comradeship.[89]

Emma Goldman and Alexander Berkman never regained the intimacy they had shared before his imprisonment, but the two revolutionaries remained close. Goldman's house at 210 East Thirteenth Street was indeed a "sort of salon" where often ideas for the next issue of *Mother Earth* were formulated. Here Emma brought Sasha, and here he eventually was able to put meaning back into his life.

Berkman became the editor of the magazine in 1908; in that position he distinguished himself with an energetic and critically acclaimed writing style for the next seven years. *Mother Earth* was more a political forum than a literary periodical; thus it did not achieve one of the goals Goldman had set for it, namely to encourage experimental literary styles. The magazine was not widely supported by writers or artists, which may have been one reason the publication was not profitable. Goldman finally had to give up her job as a masseuse and take to the lecture circuit to keep *Mother Earth* afloat.

On the Circuit Again

Between 1908 and 1917 Goldman traveled throughout the United States and made several trips to Europe to lecture and to organize protests and meetings in support of her causes. Her reputation and her influence continued to grow during this period despite U.S. government attempts to disrupt her plans. Goldman biographer Alix Shulman describes one example of the paranoia surrounding her. In 1908, after she delivered a lecture on patriotism in San Francisco, an army private, William Buwalda, shook Goldman's hand. Buwalda

> was arrested, court-martialed, dishonorably discharged, and sentenced to five years of hard labor in Alcatraz. The general who presided at the trial named his crime "shaking hands with that dangerous woman." Buwalda, a soldier for fifteen years, once decorated for "faithful service," had known nothing about anarchism at the time, but had attended Goldman's lecture out of sheer curiosity. Ten months after his sentence, he was pardoned by President Theodore Roosevelt. Upon his release from prison he sent his medal back to the army with a letter explaining he had "no further use for such baubles. . . . Give it to some one who will appreciate it more than I do." Then he joined the anarchist movement.[90]

The effort to intimidate Goldman and members of her audiences took many forms. When she neared the completion of one European trip, Goldman received word that the U.S. government was planning to deny her reentry into the country on the grounds that she had obtained her U.S. citizenship fraudulently. Goldman was not concerned, because she qualified for citizenship based on her marriage to Jacob Kershner, a naturalized American. Nonetheless she took her lawyer's advice and made her return quietly through the "back door" from Canada.

Incensed that she had avoided their trap, federal officials set out to prove that Kershner had received his citizenship illegally, which would mean that Goldman could be prosecuted. After a quick inquiry, officials decided that both the year of Kershner's birth and the year he entered the United Sates were incorrect on his application for naturalization. The judge in the case forwarded the findings to the U.S. attorney general with a notation that "this is the suit which was entered for the purpose of depriving Emma Goldman of her rights of citizenship."[91]

Federal officials then waited for their target to leave the country on another speaking tour. Goldman stayed in the United States to continue her lectures wherever she could, but an obvious pattern of harassment developed around her activities. She would book a date, and then the authorities would pressure the landlord who rented the hall or simply forbid her to speak. Quite often local groups of liberals and conservatives alike protested; they felt that Goldman's words were less harmful to society than the loss of the fundamental right of free speech would be.

The Hobo King

While Goldman toured in 1908, an economic depression affected most of the country. She planned a speech in Chicago, where many unemployed laborers had just been driven from the streets and beaten by police for demonstrating against their intolerable circumstances. City authorities there had so far been able to prevent Goldman from speaking, and she almost gave up the prospect of a meeting in Chicago. But then she learned that

Dr. Ben L. Reitman had offered us a vacant store he was using for gatherings of unemployed and hobos. We could hold our meetings there, he had said, and he had also asked to see me to discuss the matter. In the press accounts of the unemployed parade in Chicago, Reitman had been mentioned as the man who had led the march and who had been among those beaten by the police. I was curious to meet him.[92]

The "King of the Hobos," Reitman had been trained as a doctor, but had taken up the hobo life and the cause of these independent men. He was, in Goldman's words, a "handsome brute," who offered to get his hobos to clean the store they were using and prepare it for a meeting. But, as she later reported, just before the meeting was to take place,

> the store was visited by officials from the building and fire departments. They questioned the doctor as to how many he expected to seat. Sensing trouble, he said fifty. "Nine," decided the building-department. "The place is not safe for more," echoed the fire department. With one stroke our meeting was condemned, and the police scored another victory.[93]

Ben Reitman was a strange man with a dubious history, but Goldman fell in love with him almost immediately. He gave up his hobo life to take on the responsibilities of a road manager, scheduling and promoting Goldman's lectures. He had an unfortunate tendency, however, to play fast and loose with the money that was collected for the talks, and his connections to hobos with criminal backgrounds caused Goldman's friends great concern. Goldman herself writes that Reitman was exactly the sort of person she should avoid, but could not.

I could find but two explanations of the riddle: first, Ben's child-like nature, unspoiled, untrained, and utterly lacking in artifice. Whatever he said or did came spontaneously, dictated by his intensely emotional nature. It was a

In 1908 Goldman met Dr. Ben Reitman, who became the road manager for her lecture circuit.

Ben's Torture by Vigilantes

While on a speaking tour with Ben Reitman, Goldman appeared in San Diego, California, where public meetings were banned in order to prevent the Industrial Workers of the World (IWW) and other labor groups (unions) from organizing. Vigilante groups enforced the ban, and seven vigilantes with revolvers abducted Ben while he was alone in a hotel room, threatening to kill him if he made a sound. Emma Goldman includes Reitman's account of the event in her autobiography, Living My Life.

". . . Then they gathered around me. One man grabbed my right arm, another the left; a third took hold of the front of my coat, another of the back, and I was led out into the corridor, down the elevator to the ground floor of the hotel, and out into the street past a uniformed policeman, and then thrown into an automobile. When the mob saw me, they set up a howl. The auto went slowly down the main street and was joined by another one containing several persons who looked like business men. This was about half past ten in the evening. The twenty-mile ride was frightful. As soon as we got out of town, they began kicking and beating me. They took turns at pulling my long hair and they stuck their fingers into my eyes and nose. 'We could tear your guts out,' they said, 'but we promised the Chief of Police not to kill you. We are responsible men, property-owners, and the police are on our side.' When we reached the county line, the auto stopped at a deserted spot. The men formed a ring and told me to undress. They tore my clothes off. They knocked me down, and when I lay naked on the ground, they kicked and beat me until I was almost insensible. With a lighted cigar they burned the letters I.W.W. on my buttocks; then they poured a can of tar over my head and, in the absence of feathers, rubbed sage-brush on my body. One of them attempted to push a cane into my rectum. Another twisted my testicles. They forced me to kiss the flag and sing *The Star Spangled Banner*. When they tired of the fun, they gave me my underwear for fear we should meet any women. They also gave me back my vest, in order that I might carry my money, railroad ticket, and watch. The rest of my clothes they kept. I was ordered to make a speech, and then they commanded me to run the gauntlet. The Vigilantes lined up, and as I ran past them, each one gave me a blow or a kick. Then they let me go."

rare and refreshing trait, though not always pleasant in its effects. The second was my great hunger for someone who would love the woman in me and yet who would be able to also share my work. I had never had anyone who could do both.[94]

Lengthy Tours

Ben Reitman was very successful as Goldman's promoter; from 1908 to 1915 she spoke to more and larger audiences than ever before. On tours lasting up to six months each year, Reitman booked Goldman into halls in New York, throughout Pennsylvania and the Midwest, Kansas, Colorado, and California. During the last leg, she would head north through Oregon, Washington, and sometimes Canada. It was common for Goldman to lecture three to five times a week. Although she was stimulated by the debates, the questions, and even the police attempts to have her muzzled, the pace and the traveling were very strenuous.

By her own estimates Goldman spoke to between fifty and seventy-five thousand people each year at her lectures. Though anarchists, socialists, unionists, and leftists naturally were her main audience, all types of people came to hear her. A surprising number of artists, doctors, and members of social clubs made their way to the halls, because her talks ran the gamut of ideas and events of the day. She could speak on patriotism, anarchism, experimental schools, marriage, prostitution, drama and literary criticism (a popular topic), and working-class emancipation. And when the police acted to prohibit her talks, she found another place to lecture and called her address "FREE SPEECH!"

However, Goldman privately worried that her speaking efforts resulted in no more than entertainment for much of her audience. It became increasingly important to her to reach serious readers and thinkers. After all, part of the reason for the publication of *Mother Earth* and Goldman's various pamphlets was to extend exposure to her ideas beyond the lecture halls. So in late 1910, she published her first book, a collection of her lectures titled *Anarchism and Other Essays*. The book was popular not only among anarchists but also among women in the mainstream of society, many of whom for the first time read thought-provoking criticism of women's subservient role and lack of equal rights.

Another Arrest

Goldman's battles with the authorities dragged on. She continued to lecture despite occasional arrests. Typically trumped-up charges were soon dismissed and in a few days she would be back on the platform giving the same passionate addresses.

One of her lectures focused on birth control, a practice that had been outlawed in the United States in connection with the so-called Comstock Laws of 1873 aimed at suppressing all kinds of material deemed obscene. Even though large numbers of women practiced some type of birth control by the early 1900s, federal law forbade both the use of contraceptives, or birth control devices, and the spread of information about them.

Goldman supported the work of Margaret Sanger, who had become well known

By 1916, when this photograph was taken, Goldman had endured several arrests as a result of her anarchist views.

alter her focus dramatically. World War I, brought on by German-led aggression on many fronts, was raging throughout Europe. The United States had remained neutral for as long as it was politically feasible. But by 1917 many Americans believed that their country had to prepare for the inevitable. The federal government authorized a huge buildup of arms and war matériel and also instituted a conscription, or draft, of all eligible male citizens to organize and train an army.

A vast majority of the populace supported the war effort by this time, but support was not universal. A vocal minority protested their government's intent to

Goldman supported the work of birth control advocate Margaret Sanger (pictured).

for her efforts to educate women about family planning and contraceptives. Goldman also lectured frequently on the need to challenge the law against distributing contraceptive information, arguing that birth control was no criminal offense. "I have simply given to the poorer women in my audiences information that any wealthy woman can obtain secretly from her physician, who does not fear prosecution. I have offered them advice as to how to escape the burden of large families without resorting to illegal operations."[95]

Although Goldman was committed to the issue of women's reproductive rights, changing events in Europe caused her to

Officials look on as Secretary of War Newton Baker draws the names of World War I draftees. Goldman vehemently opposed the draft and spoke publicly against it.

join the fray, and many objected to conscription.

Goldman was morally opposed to the idea of war, and she argued that men sent to die for their country were acting as the slaves of the upper classes, who were actually enriching themselves in these "patriotic" efforts. "The pathos of it all," she writes, "is that the America which is to be protected by a huge military force is not the America of the people, but that of the privileged class; the class which robs and exploits the masses, and controls their lives from the cradle to the grave."[96]

She was especially opposed to the idea of conscription because it ignored individual choice. She felt that a man should have the right to decide to fight—if he was so inclined. But with the draft, the government determined the behavior of the people, and that was in direct opposition to Goldman's anarchist philosophy.

The No-Conscription League

In May of 1917 she created the No-Conscription League to counsel and support

Goldman and Berkman, shown together in a 1918 photo, joined forces to organize mass rallies to protest the draft. Most Americans considered Goldman and Berkman's views unpatriotic.

those men who opposed the draft. With Alexander Berkman, she organized mass rallies, once speaking to more than eight thousand people. *Mother Earth* carried articles on the league's philosophy and activities, and the mainstream press reprinted excerpts. Goldman, always controversial, became even more infamous. In their patriotic zeal, most Americans felt no sympathy for what they believed was Goldman's treasonous point of view. And the government agreed.

On June 15, 1917, Emma and Sasha were arrested for their antidraft activities. The marshal who came to her offices had no warrant and no authority to confiscate her papers but, as was typical of police dealings with Goldman, was intent only on silencing her regardless of correct legal procedure. Bail was set at a very high $25,000, and Goldman was not allowed to convert liberty bonds or to have friends' property put up as collateral to meet the cash requirement.

Both Goldman and Berkman were resigned to the fact that the government was going to have its way with them, even though the conscription law was not in effect when they held the meeting that was the basis of the charges against them. They decided that the best course of action was to speak out, as they had always

No Conscription!

Opposed to militarism and the draft of young men to fight in World War I, Emma Goldman and Alexander Berkman helped organize the No-Conscription League, which issued a manifesto in 1917. These excerpts from the manifesto are included in The Life and Times of Emma Goldman *by Goldman scholar Candace Falk.*

"Conscription has now become a fact in this country. It took England fully 18 months after she engaged in the war to impose compulsory military service on her people. It was left for 'free' America to pass a conscription bill six weeks after she declared war against Germany.

What becomes of the patriotic boast of America to have entered the European war in behalf of the principle of democracy? But that is not all. Every country in Europe has recognized the right of conscientious objectors—of men who refuse to engage in war on the ground that they are opposed to taking life. Yet this democratic country makes no such provision for those who will not commit murder at the behest of the war profiteers. Thus, the 'land of the free and the home of the brave' is ready to coerce free men into the military yoke. . . .

Liberty of conscience is the most fundamental of all human rights. . . .

The NO-CONSCRIPTION LEAGUE has been formed for the purpose of encouraging conscientious objectors to affirm their liberty of conscience and to make their objection to human slaughter effective by refusing to participate in the killing of their fellow men. . . . Our platform may be summarized as follows:

We oppose conscription because we are internationalists, anti-militarists, and opposed to all wars waged by capitalistic governments.

We will fight for what we choose to fight for; we will never fight simply because we are ordered to fight.

We believe that the militarization of America is an evil that far outweighs, in its anti-social and anti-libertarian effects, any good that may come from America's participation in the war.

We will resist conscription by every means in our power, and we will sustain those who, for similar reasons, refuse to be conscripted."

done, for their ideals and the cause. Acting as their own attorneys at their trial, both defendants spoke eloquently of the reasons why their presence at such a proceeding was a miscarriage of justice.

In her final address, Goldman appealed to the jury for justice:

> When Thoreau was placed in prison for refusing to pay taxes, he was visited by Ralph Waldo Emerson and Emerson said: "David, what are you doing in jail?" and Thoreau replied: "Ralph, what are you doing outside, when honest people are in jail for their ideals?" Gentlemen of the jury, I do not wish to appeal to your passions. I do not wish to influence you by the fact that I am a woman. . . . I take it that you are sincere enough and honest enough to render a verdict according to your convictions, beyond the shadow of a reasonable doubt.
>
> Please forget that we are Anarchists. Forget that it is claimed that we propagated violence. Forget that something appeared in *Mother Earth* when I was thousands of miles away, three years ago. Forget all that, and merely consider the evidence. . . . Your verdict must be not guilty.
>
> But whatever your decision, the struggle must go on. We are but the atoms in the incessant human struggle towards the light that shines in the darkness—the Ideal of economic, political and spiritual liberation of mankind![97]

In spite of Goldman's plea, the jury deliberated only thirty-nine minutes before returning a guilty verdict. The judge imposed a harsh sentence of two years in prison and a $10,000 fine. He also recommended deportation.

Harry Weinberger, a lawyer who had helped Goldman in other encounters with the police, filed an appeal to overturn the convictions of Goldman and Berkman, but the U.S. Supreme Court denied the move. Sasha began serving a two-year sentence in an Atlanta, Georgia, prison, while Emma was sentenced to serve her time in the penitentiary at Jefferson City, Missouri, at the time the largest prison in the United States.

Lawyer Harry Weinberger (left), who had helped Goldman in the past, was unable to convince the Court to overturn its decision against Goldman for her antidraft activities.

Prison Life

Of the twenty-three hundred people incarcerated at Jefferson City, only about one hundred were women, whom Goldman describes as "poor wretches of the world of poverty and drabness. Coloured or white, most of them had been driven to crime by conditions that had greeted them at birth. . . . I found no criminals among them, but only unfortunates, broken, hapless, and hopeless human beings."[98]

Every woman who entered the Jefferson City facility was forced to give up her street clothing for a cheap, rough-textured, brown muslin dress. The place was overcrowded, filthy, and harshly administered. Each seven-by-eight-foot cell had an iron bunk on which was placed one bag of straw for a mattress and another for a pillow. A table and a chair, a toilet, and a sink with running water were included in the sparse living space. The dining hall was cockroach infested.

When Goldman entered the prison in 1918, she was forty-nine years old and not in good health. Her physical ailments were aggravated by the demanding work that was required of all inmates: sewing jackets, overalls, and suspenders for nine hours each day. Since Goldman was nearsighted, she had to bend over to see the stitches, causing acute neck and back pains. In her autobiography, Emma describes how the shop system worked:

Two months were allowed to learn the trade. . . . The tasks varied from forty-five to a hundred and twenty-one jackets a day, or from nine to eighteen dozen suspenders. While the actual machine work on the different tasks was the same, some of them required double physical exertion. The full complement of work was demanded without regard to age or physical condition. Even illness, unless of a very serious nature, was not considered sufficient cause for relieving the worker. . . .

The shop was dreaded by all the inmates, particularly on account of the foreman. He was a boy of twenty-one who had been in charge of the treadmill since he was sixteen. An ambitious young man, he was very clever in pressing the tasks out of the women. If insults failed, the threat of punishment brought results. The women were so terrorized by him that they rarely dared to speak up. If anyone did, she became his special target for persecution. He was not even averse to robbing them of a part of their work and then reporting them for impudence, thus increasing their punishment for being short of the task.[99]

Along with this "official bully" of the system, "Captain Gilvan, the acting warden, and Lilah Smith, the head matron, made up the triple alliance in control of the prison régime," Emma writes. Gilvan forbade any woman to leave her work without permission and, with the aid of the matron, used various forms of punishment to keep his prisoners in line. Sometimes he locked women in their cells for forty-eight hours on a bread-and-water diet or put prisoners in a "blind cell," which was entirely dark and measured only four-by-eight feet, for up to three weeks. Gilvan also punished inmates by hanging them from their wrists and bellowing that they "must make the task . . .

no such thing as 'can't.' I punish cheerfully, mark you that!"[100]

Although she had a difficult time in prison, Goldman nevertheless tended to the needs of the other inmates, a trait that was inherent in her character. When Goldman's friends were able to send food to her, she shared the treats with other prisoners and even with the guards. She spoke on behalf of inmates with prison authorities, obtained reading material for them, and generally mothered the ones she saw as uneducated and unfortunate.

While Emma was imprisoned, many others who opposed militarism and the draft were arrested and sentenced to long prison terms. Some were anarchists or members of labor unions. Others were socialists opposed to a war effort they saw as capitalist. Kate Richard O'Hare, a famous socialist who later became a prison reformer, was installed in a cell next to Goldman's. O'Hare had been sentenced to five years in prison for delivering an antiwar speech.

Although Emma and Kate did not always agree on political issues, they became good friends. When Goldman was released from prison, O'Hare wrote this assessment of her companion, stressing Goldman's maternal instincts: "Thwarted in physical motherhood she poured out her whole soul in vicarious motherhood of all the sad and sorrowful, the wronged and oppressed, the bitter and rebellious children of men. Warden Gilvan was right when he said the women here worshipped her."[101]

But Emma Goldman showed more than compassion for inmates who were imprisoned because of what she termed a "mad" social structure. She was also determined to demonstrate that the government could not silence her.

While in prison in 1918, Goldman found a friend in socialist Kate Richard O'Hare, who was serving time for antiwar activities.

Release and a Final Tour

After serving their time in prison Goldman and Berkman were reunited and planned a speaking tour of the United States. They hoped to raise money for a legal suit challenging a series of government raids on leftists and anarchist activists, in which police had arrested and confined people without formal charges.

At this time government officials, fearful that the effects of the successful 1917 communist revolution in Russia would carry over to the United States, saw "conspiracies" everywhere. This fear of a communist takeover (or "red scare," as it was called) prompted some citizens to accuse others of being "un-American." The label was applied to people whose writings, lectures, or participation in any activity seemed to be sympathetic to the communists who overthrew the Russian czar. Anyone labeled un-American was at risk of being jailed or deported.

Goldman suspected that her days in the United States were numbered. The director of the Federal Bureau of Investigation (FBI), J. Edgar Hoover, and other federal officials had worked hard to build a legal case to deport Goldman as well as

With communist suspicions on the rise in the United States, Goldman became the target of the FBI's deportation attempts.

Berkman. In a memorandum Hoover wrote on August 23, 1919, to the special assistant to the attorney general, he concluded that "Emma Goldman and Alexander Berkman are, beyond doubt, two of the most dangerous anarchists in this country and if permitted to return to the community will result in undue harm."[102]

No Recourse

Since the federal government had successfully denaturalized Emma's husband, Jacob Kershner, denying his U.S. citizenship, Emma was considered an alien, and the recently passed Immigration Act of 1918 made it possible to deport or exclude aliens who engaged in anarchist activities. Kershner's rightful citizenship could not be contested because he was presumed dead. So Goldman had no recourse.

As for Berkman, there was no argument. He did not claim U.S. citizenship, calling himself a citizen of the world, and he would not denounce his belief in anarchism.

At first Goldman tried to appeal her case, but realizing that her friend, now ill and weak, would have to make the trip back across the Atlantic alone, Emma decided to accept her fate. They were both ordered to appear at Ellis Island before noon on December 5, 1919. There they waited, incarcerated once more, until a ship was ready to take them out of the country.

8 Life in Exile

Goldman spent her time at Ellis Island writing essays, manifestos protesting the injustice of her deportation, and personal letters to comrades she would not see again. She sent a heartfelt note to Ben Reitman, urging him to keep her memory alive, and thanking him for his love over the years.

> I was glad to have been in Chicago and to see you again, dearest Hobo. . . . During our years together, I have done my best and most valuable work. My two books, the continuance of ME during all the years. I owe them to you. Your devotion, your untiring work, your tremendous energy. If I owe also much heartache—much soul-tearing misery to you, what of it. Nothing great in life can be achieved without pain. I am glad to have paid the price. I can only hope I too have given you something worth whatever price you have paid for your love. I shall feel proud & glad.[103]

Deportation

Convinced that it had captured all of the leaders of the anarchist movement, the government prepared to rid the country of "evil." On December 21, 1919, before sunrise on that cold, Sunday morning, New York state and federal officials ordered the radical immigrants imprisoned on Ellis Island to line up. Then the group of 249 was marched through the snow to a barge that would carry them to the S.S.

Labeled with a number for identification, Goldman awaits her deportation at Ellis Island in 1919.

Addressing the Jury

When Goldman and Berkman went to trial on conspiracy charges, they chose to defend themselves. This excerpt from Goldman's address to the jury is found in Red Emma Speaks: Selected Writings and Speeches by Emma Goldman, *edited by Alix Shulman.*

"On the day after our arrest it was given out by the U.S. Marshal and the District Attorney's office that the 'big fish' of the No-Conscription activities had been caught, and that there would be no more trouble-makers and disturbers to interfere with the highly democratic effort of the Government to conscript its young manhood for the European slaughter. . . .

The methods employed by Marshal McCarthy and his hosts of heroic warriors were sensational enough to satisfy the famous circus men, Barnum & Bailey. A dozen or more heroes dashing up two flights of stairs, prepared to stake their lives for their country, only to discover the two dangerous disturbers and trouble-makers, Alexander Berkman and Emma Goldman, in their separate offices, quietly at work at their desks, wielding not a sword, nor a gun or a bomb, but merely their pens! Verily, it required courage to catch such big fish. . . .

In their zeal to save the country from the trouble-makers, the Marshal and his helpers did not even consider it necessary to produce a search warrant. After all, what matters a mere scrap of paper when one is called upon to raid the offices of Anarchists! Of what consequence is the sanctity of property, the right of privacy, to officials in their dealings with Anarchists! In our day of military training for battle, an Anarchist office is an appropriate camping ground. Would the gentlemen who came with Marshal McCarthy have dared to go into the offices of Morgan, or Rockefeller, or of any of those men without a search warrant? . . . They turned our office into a battlefield, so that when they were through with it, it looked like invaded Belgium, with the only difference that the invaders were not Prussian barbarians but good American patriots bent on making New York safe for democracy."

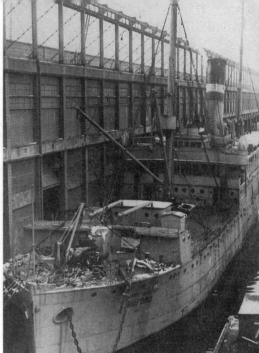

Judged as threats to the U.S. government, Goldman, Berkman, and other anarchists board the S.S. Buford *(right), which will transport them to Russia.*

Buford, a troop transport ship used in the Spanish-American War.

Goldman and the two other women deportees, with guards in front of and behind them, were the last to cross the gangplank to the barge. They were sent to a cabin belowdecks. Then the barge lurched away from the dock. As Goldman described the scene years later:

> I looked at my watch. It was 4:20 A.M. . . . On the deck above us I could hear the men tramping up and down in the wintry blast. I felt dizzy, visioning a transport of politicals doomed to Siberia. . . . Russia of the past rose before me and I saw the revolutionary martyrs being driven into exile. But no, it was New York, it was America, the land of liberty! Through the port-hole I could see the great city receding into the distance, its sky-line of buildings traceable by their rearing heads. It was my beloved city, the metropolis of the New World. It was America, indeed, America repeating the terrible scenes of tsarist Russia! I glanced up—the Statue of Liberty![104]

Although being deported from the United States deeply saddened and disappointed Emma Goldman, she was able to reflect on the irony of this turn of events. So many years earlier she had escaped the oppressive czarist state of Russia to find personal freedom in America. Now the oppressive policies of her adopted land were responsible for her involuntary exile to a Russia that she believed had just won a hard-fought revolution over that same sort of tyranny.

Life aboard the old ship was extremely difficult. The *Buford* was battered and unseaworthy, and the hold of the ship, where all the men—including Berkman—were confined, was cold and damp, with no ventilation. They had only saltwater for washing and only two toilets for 246 men. As Goldman writes:

> Many of the deportees had been given no opportunity to provide themselves with warm clothing, and there was much suffering as a result. Sasha suggested that those who had supplies should share what they could spare with their less fortunate comrades, and the men responded beautifully. Bags, suit-cases, and trunks were unpacked, everyone donating whatever he did not absolutely require for himself. Coats, underwear, hats, socks, and other apparel were piled up in one of the compartments below deck, and a commission was selected for distribution. The story of the proceedings, as told to me by Sasha, [showed] the splendid solidarity and fellow-feeling of the deportees.[105]

For most of the voyage Goldman tried to focus on the new life she expected to find in Mother Russia. In 1917 the Bolsheviks, a party of communist extremists, had overthrown the czar by violent revolution. Led by Vladimir Ilich Ulyanov Lenin, the Bolsheviks were establishing a new Soviet Union. Goldman looked forward to the landing but she also expressed concern that she and Berkman might not be welcome.

Russian troops fire on the fearless Bolsheviks at a demonstration against czarist rule in July 1917. Just a few months later, the Bolsheviks would grab national power and start a new regime.

Disillusionment with Russia

The *Buford* docked in Finland, and from there the deportees traveled by train to the Russian border. Before they could cross the border they had to convince Soviet guards that they were not invaders—a task that fell to Berkman, who was able to explain in Russian the group's circumstances. The guards told them a committee was forming to meet them, and

---

A Silent Hearing

When immigration officials held a hearing and attempted to "prove" that Goldman had a criminal past, she refused to take part or answer questions. Instead she handed her examiners a prepared statement, which she includes in Living My Life. *It read in part:*

"If the present proceedings are for the purpose of proving some alleged offence committed by me, some evil or antisocial act, then I protest against the secrecy and third-degree methods of this so-called 'trial.' But if I am not charged with any specific offence or act, if—as I have reason to believe—this is purely an inquiry into my social and political opinions, then I protest still more vigorously against these proceedings, as utterly tyrannical and diametrically opposed to the fundamental guarantees of a true democracy. Every human being is entitled to hold any opinion that appeals to her or him without making herself or himself liable to persecution. . . .

The free expression of the hopes and aspirations of a people is the greatest and only safety in a sane society. In truth, it is such free expression and discussion alone that can point the most beneficial path for human progress and development. But the object of deportations and of the Anti-Anarchist Law, as of all similar repressive measures, is the very opposite. It is to stifle the voice of the people, to muzzle every aspiration of labour. That is the real and terrible menace of the star-chamber proceedings and of the tendency of exiling those who do not fit into the scheme of things our industrial lords are so eager to perpetuate.

With all the power and intensity of my being I protest against the conspiracy of imperialist capitalism against the life and the liberty of the American people.

Emma Goldman."

eventually they were escorted across the border accompanied by a military band.

The deportees were greeted like honored comrades. Goldman describes the scene:

> We who had been driven out of America as felons were welcomed on Soviet soil as brothers by her sons and daughters who had helped to set her free. Workers, soldiers, and peasants surrounded us, took us by the hand, and made us feel akin to them.
>
> Music and song greeted us everywhere and wondrous tales of valour and never-failing fortitude in the face of hunger, cold, and devastating disease. Tears of gratitude burned in my eyes and I felt great humility before those simple folk risen to greatness in the fire of the revolutionary struggle.[106]

However, Goldman soon became aware of Bolshevik atrocities, of executions of counterrevolutionaries by the hundreds. During one meeting of laborers, Emma heard cries of

> anguish and bitterness against the people they had helped place in power. They spoke of the Bolshevik betrayal of the Revolution, of the slavery forced upon the toilers . . . the suppression of speech and thought, the filling of prisons with . . . peasants, workers, soldiers, sailors, and rebels . . . and the wholesale executions without hearing or trial.[107]

Goldman did not want to believe what she heard and saw—evidence that the revolutionaries, once in power, had become tyrants different only in name. This certainly was not the beginning of a new free

Russian author Maksim Gorky called revolution "a grim and relentless task."

society. Distressed and unsure how to proceed, she discussed her concerns with Sasha. But Berkman was ill at the time, and dismissed complaints against the Bolsheviks as silly gossip.

Voicing Her Complaints

Goldman sought advice from friends, union leaders, and others. She once talked with Maksim Gorky, a well-known Russian author and spokesman for the revolution, who reminded her that "revolution is a grim and relentless task." He had little sympathy for the masses, whom he called "uncivilized" with "no cultural traditions, no social values, no respect for human rights and life. They cannot be moved by anything except coercion and force." Goldman "protested vehemently against these charges," and argued that the Russian peasants were the first to revolt. But Gorky claimed that Lenin, the great Bolshevik leader, was the "real parent" of the revolution.[108]

Emma began to write down all the contradictions she found in Soviet life and convinced Sasha to help her present her views to Lenin. Although Berkman felt that temporary abuses were justified and necessary in the establishment of a new order, he agreed to visit Lenin with her. After hearing her complaints, Lenin told her "Russia was making giant strides at home and abroad. It was igniting the world revolution," and he chastised Goldman for "lamenting over a little blood-letting."[109]

Dismayed, Goldman thought about leaving the country. But she was torn between her loyalty to the revolutionary cause and her instinctive desire to remedy the injustices that prevailed. She wondered what work she could do to help her fellow Russians.

An answer came when she joined a group of researchers who were traveling throughout Russia to gather material of historical value for a new museum. The institution was to be dedicated to preserving the history of the 1917 revolution. Goldman found she could separate her admiration for that struggle from her dislike of the government that was created afterwards. This rationalization allowed her to stay true to her ideals and stay in Russia. The assignment also allowed her an opportunity to travel among the people to assess conditions firsthand.

Later she analyzed the economics of the society to conclude that Russia did not even approach the theoretical ideal of the communist model the revolution was supposed to have made possible.

The essence of Communism, even of the coercive kind, is the absence of social classes. The introduction of social equality is the first step. . . . Even at the risk of condemnation for telling the whole truth, I must state unequivocally and unconditionally that the very opposite is the case in Soviet Russia. Bolshevism has not abolished the classes in Russia: it merely reversed their former relationship. . . . When I arrived in Soviet Russia in January, 1920, I found innumerable economic categories, based on the food rations received from the government. The sailor was getting the best ration. . . . He was the aristocrat of the Revolution. . . . After him came the soldier. . . . Below the soldier in the scale was the worker in the military industries; then came other workers, subdivided into the skilled, the artisan, the laborer, etc. . . . Members of the former bourgeoisie, officially abolished as a class and expropriated, were in the last economic category and received practically nothing.[110]

The Final Straw

In the early months of 1921 workers in Petrograd (Saint Petersburg) staged a massive strike, protesting their grinding poverty, lack of fuel, and the many privileges that the ruling class enjoyed. Bolshevik leaders ordered the workers to return to their jobs, but the strikers refused. Many were arrested and imprisoned. Nonetheless the strike spread to other cities, and sailors meeting in Kronstadt joined the protest, demanding free speech and a free press. Fearing loss of control, Lenin ordered the army to put down the protest, and tens of thousands of people were massacred.

This terrible slaughter convinced even Berkman that the Bolshevik leadership had taken the wrong direction. He and Goldman decided to find a way to leave Russia once more. They knew that a request to emigrate would be denied; government authorities were afraid that, given access to the world press, Emma and Sasha would spread damaging criticism of the revolutionary government. Luckily, an invitation came asking both of them to attend an anarchist convention in Berlin, Germany. After much delay, the authori-

ties granted visas, and Emma and Sasha prepared to leave.

"In the train, December 1, 1921!" she writes. "My dreams crushed, my faith broken, my heart like a stone. *Matushka Rossiya* [Mother Russia] bleeding from a thousand wounds, her soil strewn with the dead. I clutch the bar at the frozen window-pane and grit my teeth to suppress my sobs."[111] After two years in their homeland, Emma and Sasha would now be people without a country.

Years of Wandering

For a time Emma and Sasha made a home in Stockholm, Sweden, and both began writing about their experience in Russia, publishing an article in a major Swedish

Goldman and Berkman (far left) with friends in Stockholm, Sweden, where the couple lived after leaving Russia in 1921.

newspaper and granting interviews to journalists. But Swedish officials soon barred their articles from Swedish publications. Goldman reasoned that this was because "Sweden was at the time discussing the recognition of the Russian Government."[112]

However, the New York *World* was willing to pay $2,100 for a seven-part series of articles on Goldman's impressions of the Soviet government and the people of Russia. With the advance for that writing assignment, she was able to travel with Berkman to Germany in 1922. There they both concentrated on producing book-length works on their Russian experience. Goldman's *My Two Years in Russia* was eventually published as *My Disillusionment in Russia*. It was mistakenly printed without the final twelve chapters, but no reviewer seemed to notice that the book ended in midstream. However, her criticism of the revolution brought her negative reaction in Europe and Goldman was forced to leave Germany.

In July 1924 Emma went to England, hoping that she could again resume her anarchist activities. Unfortunately she found that her book had generated much resentment among the British liberal movement. And when a British trade union group returned from Moscow with glowing reports of conditions there under the Bolsheviks, she was further ostracized. At a loss for an outlet in which to apply her still considerable energies, she turned to another of her passionate interests: drama.

Since her days with Johann Most and her exposure to the classics with Ed Brady, she had studied, written, and discussed the arts and drama. While touring the United States between 1908 and 1916, some of her most successful lectures had dealt with dramatic criticism. She had

A 1925 handbill advertises one of Goldman's lectures on the arts.

kept up with modern developments in the theater, so a lecture series drawing on her knowledge seemed like a natural choice.

The talks were not financially successful, however. This fact and the frustration of not being able to speak out in public because she was an alien led her into a marriage of convenience with a longtime anarchist friend. In June 1925 Goldman married Welsh coal miner James Colton. The marriage gave Goldman protection as a British subject under English law. But this tactic did not enhance her opportunities much within England, so she made plans to travel to the south of France.

"A Shrewd Politician"

While in exile in Russia, Emma Goldman became highly critical of Lenin, father of the revolution, calling him "a shrewd politician who knew exactly what he was about and . . . would stop at nothing to achieve his ends." Emma published her views as an afterword for My Disillusionment in Russia, *and Alix Shulman includes it in* Red Emma Speaks: Selected Writings and Speeches by Emma Goldman.

"After hearing him speak on several occasions and reading his works I became convinced that Lenin had very little concern in the revolution and that Communism to him was a very remote thing. The centralized political State was Lenin's deity, to which everything else was to be sacrificed. Someone said that Lenin would sacrifice the Revolution to save Russia. Lenin's policies, however, have proven that he was willing to sacrifice both the Revolution and the country; or at least part of the latter, in order to realize his political scheme with what was left of Russia.

Lenin was the most pliable politician in history. He could be an ultra-revolutionary, a compromiser and conservative at the same time. When like a mighty wave the cry swept over Russia 'All power to the Soviets!' Lenin swam with the tide. When the peasants took possession of the land and the workers of the factories, Lenin not only approved of those direct methods but went further. He issued the famous motto, 'Rob the robbers,' a slogan which served to confuse the minds of the people and caused untold injury to revolutionary idealism. Never before did any real revolutionist interpret social expropriation as the transfer of wealth from one set of individuals to another. Yet that was exactly what Lenin's slogan meant. The indiscriminate and irresponsible raids, the accumulation of the wealth of the former bourgeoisie by the new Soviet bureaucracy, the chicanery practised toward those whose only crime was their former status, were all the results of Lenin's 'Rob the robbers' policy. The whole subsequent history of the Revolution is a kaleidoscope of Lenin's compromises and betrayal of his own slogans."

Goldman questioned Lenin's motives in leading the Russian Revolution.

Bon Esprit

Some of Goldman's friends had purchased a small cottage, called "Bon Esprit," for her in Saint-Tropez on the French Riviera, where she settled in, hoping to earn some money from writing. She had received an advance to complete an essay on Johann Most, but that money would not go far. She also had done quite a bit of research on the history of Russian drama, and she had a commitment from a British publisher for a book on the subject, but the deal fell through when the English economy took a downturn. Forced to do what she had always done when she was in need of cash, Goldman returned to the lecture circuit.

This time she was booked to tour throughout Canada. She had to borrow money from some American friends to pay for her passage. Her organizers were inexperienced and her first lectures were poorly attended. Had it not been for the publicity provided by a Toronto newspaper reporter, C. R. Reade, the whole endeavor might have been a disaster. Once the tour was under way, however, Goldman exhibited the same energy she had displayed in the old days. In Edmonton, Alberta, for example, she delivered fifteen lectures in a week, and up to three speeches in a single day. Her audiences were "variegated," ranging from "factory girls" to whom she spoke "during their lunch hour in the shop" to "the faculties of Edmonton College and the University of Alberta," who listened to Goldman at a fancy tea in a hotel.[113]

Goldman completed the fifteen-month tour energized and excited about the possibilities for the future. And she had a little money to return to her cottage and concentrate on her autobiography. "I was returning to France, to lovely Saint-Tropez and my enchanting little cottage to write my life. My life—I had lived in its heights and its depths, in bitter sorrow and ecstatic joy, in black despair and fervent hope. I had drunk the cup to the last drop. I had lived my life. Would I had the gift to paint the life I had lived."[114]

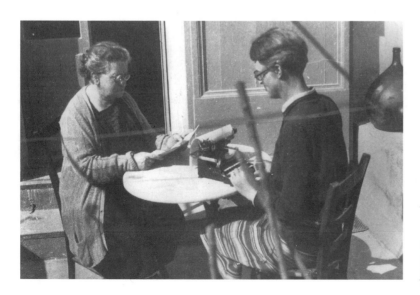

Goldman dictates her memoirs to a secretary in Saint-Tropez, France.

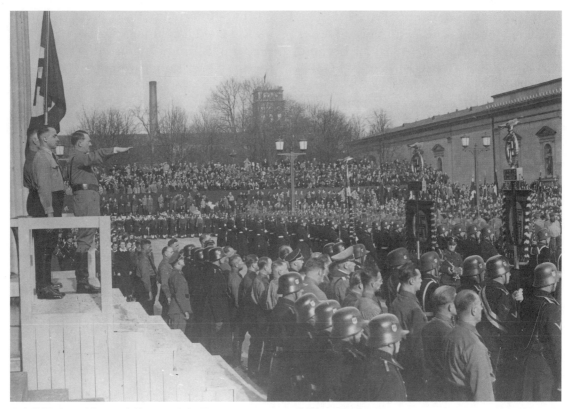

Adolf Hitler addresses followers of the Fascist movement. Goldman, who was outspoken in her criticism of Hitler, warned her audiences of his potential danger.

Living My Life

Her return to France in 1928 marked the beginning of a less hectic period in Goldman's life. Money worries still plagued her, however, and she was concerned about Sasha, who was in poor health and had no regular income, living day-to-day in an apartment in nearby Nice. But her new cause was to complete her life story, and with Berkman's help that is what she concentrated on for the next three years.

When Goldman's autobiography was published in 1931, the two-volume set of *Living My Life* sold for $7.50. Goldman thought that the price was too high for the working-class reader she expected would be her main audience. Whether the reason was the pricing or the worldwide economic depression, the book sold poorly. Goldman and Berkman, deeply disappointed, had counted on some financial security with the publication of the manuscript.

Goldman continued to lecture where she could in Europe, now often warning her audiences about the growing menace of the Fascists of Italy and Germany, who declared that their countries and people were superior to all others. In 1932, traveling through Scandinavian countries, she lectured on the dangers of Adolf Hitler and his bloodhounds, who were gaining power in Germany. When Hitler became the dictator of Germany in 1933, Goldman over and over again urged people in Holland and other European countries to beware the iron hand of Hitler and his Nazis and their threat to take over all of Europe. Because of her outspoken criticism of Hitler, she was expelled from Holland; the country feared it would become one of Hitler's targets and was reluctant to antagonize Germany.

Goldman faced similar fears and rebuffs in other European countries, and she returned to her cottage in France feeling rejected and depressed. She longed to return to Canada or the United States for one more tour, hoping to renew ties with people she knew and loved in America.

The American Civil Liberties Union backed Goldman in her efforts to return to the United States. Along with the help of leading liberals and prominent American writers such as Sinclair Lewis, Dorothy Canfield Fisher, and Theodore Dreiser, a ninety-day speaking tour was arranged. The government agreed to provide a visa on one condition: the only topics Goldman could address were literature and drama.

Goldman, predictably, balked, because she intended some of her first speeches to be on political issues, especially on the dangers posed by Hitler's regime and other dictatorships. Eventually she was able to reach an agreement stating that she would define what was literature and drama once she reached the United States. Thus on February 1, 1934, Emma Goldman sailed into New York Harbor one more time.

9 Endings

"On coming to America I had the same hopes as have most European immigrants and the same disillusionment, though the latter affected me more keenly and more deeply," writes Emma Goldman in a magazine article published in 1934 after she returned to her adopted land. Goldman goes on to summarize her experiences:

> I soon learned that in a republic there are myriad ways by which the strong, the cunning, the rich can seize power and hold it. I saw the many work for small wages which kept them always on want for the few who made huge profits. I saw the courts, the halls of legislation, the press, and the schools . . . effectively used as an instrument for the safeguarding of a minority, while the masses were denied every right. I found that the politicians knew how to befog every issue, how to control public opinion and manipulate votes to their own advantage and to that of their financial and industrial allies. This was the picture of democracy I soon discovered on my arrival in the United States. Fundamentally there have been few changes since that time.[115]

As Emma Goldman's words made clear, she had long ago put aside illusions about any government's ability to function

After spending fifteen years in exile, Goldman returned to the United States to begin a lecture tour. Here, she is greeted by her niece upon her arrival in New York in 1934.

without harming the people it had been established to protect. Returning to the United States in 1934 after fifteen years of exile, she once again turned to the possibility of devoting herself to the cause of anarchism and individual freedom. As she told a news crew when she reached U.S.

shores, "Only liberty is worth fighting for. This is the job I'll keep at until I am either hanged or fall asleep in some other way."[116]

The Final Tour

The Goldman name and quotes from Emma still helped sell newspapers, and Goldman was well received in New York City and Rochester, but in other cities the lecture halls did not fill up for the veteran activist's final speaking tour. She alienated a large portion of her potential audience of leftists and liberals because she strongly objected to communism and fascism, which North American radicals supported. She had seen the theories put into practice in Europe, and she was horrified by the results. But American audiences of 1934 found her warnings obsolete or irrelevant and the tour ended up a financial disaster.

Regardless of the audience response Goldman was excited and full of life back in her old environment. One Madison, Wisconsin, editorial pointed out:

> The intelligence and vitality of Emma Goldman impressed deeply her four hundred hearers in Madison. Old, but ageless, she radiated what the charm-school ads call "personality." . . . Battered by life, life flows from her, steadily, hotly; her blood and passion are the weapons she has dedicated to her revolutionary cause.[117]

Goldman even asked for an extension of her visa from immigration officials. But they refused her request and soon she was sailing sadly back to France. She had come to realize that she would spend the remainder of her life as an alien abroad.

Farewell to Berkman

The next two years were rough ones for the two old anarchists. Berkman was ill with cancer and almost always depressed. He could not earn a decent wage for his work as a translator or ghostwriter. Goldman did what she could to supplement his income, but her earnings were also meager. The one thing that she did have to give Sasha was her abiding love.

In a birthday message that she wrote to him in 1935, she confessed how much he meant to her:

> As a greeting to your sixty-fifth birthday it is fitting that I should tell you

A poster advertises Goldman's 1934 lecture in New Haven, Connecticut. The audience response to Goldman's tour was less than enthusiastic.

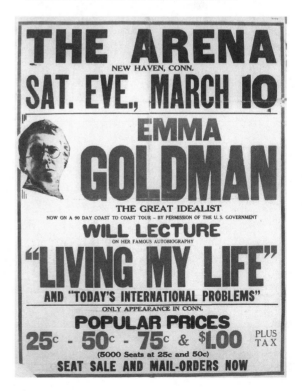

Women's Issues

Long before it was acceptable to do so, Emma Goldman discussed "women's issues" in public forums, presenting her ideas on controversial topics including birth control and sexuality. In the essay "Marriage and Love," collected in Red Emma Speaks: Selected Writings and Speeches by Emma Goldman, *edited by Alix Shulman, Goldman declares:*

"From infancy, almost, the average girl is told that marriage is her ultimate goal; therefore her training and education must be directed towards that end. Like the mute beast fattened for slaughter, she is prepared for that. Yet, strange to say, she is allowed to know much less about her function as wife and mother than the ordinary artisan of his trade. It is indecent and filthy for a respectable girl to know anything of the marital relation. Oh, for the inconsistency of respectability, that needs the marriage vow to turn something which is filthy into the purest and most sacred arrangement that none dare question or criticize. Yet that is exactly the attitude of the average upholder of marriage. The prospective wife and mother is kept in complete ignorance of her only asset in the competitive field—sex. Thus she enters into life-long relations with a man only to find herself shocked, repelled, outraged beyond measure by the most natural and healthy instinct, sex. It is safe to say that a large percentage of the unhappiness, misery, distress, and physical suffering of matrimony is due to the criminal ignorance in sex matters that is being extolled as a great virtue. Nor is it all an exaggeration when I say that more than one home has been broken up because of this deplorable fact."

the secret of my life. It is that the one treasure I have rescued from my long and bitter struggle is my friendship for you. . . . No one ever was so rooted in my being, so ingrained in my every fiber, as you have been and are to this day. Men have come and gone in my long life. But you, my dearest will remain forever. . . . I know that the only loss that would matter would be to lose your friendship.[118]

Even though they disagreed on many issues, for more than forty years Emma and Sasha were bound as comrades in the cause and by a deep love between two passionate souls. Even during his many years in prison, Berkman and Goldman were still together in spirit. Thus it was devastating for Emma when, exhausted by his depression and in agonizing pain from cancer, Sasha decided he had had enough. He shot himself, aiming for but missing his heart. Rushed to a hospital, Berkman died sixteen hours later, on June 28, 1936. A grieving Goldman wrote to a friend:

> I once thought I would always find strength to overcome the greatest shocks. I confess I find myself lacking in the very quality my friend admired most, courage and fortitude. . . .
>
> And yet I shall and must go on. If only to articulate to the world the personality and spirit that was Alexander Berkman. . . . Just now I am far from detached enough for anything that would do justice to my friend. Perhaps later, when the wound has left but a deep scar, I pray I may have the ability and the objectivity to give Alexander Berkman to posterity.[119]

The Spanish Civil War

Goldman's depression over Berkman's suicide deepened and she appeared to have little will to live. But thankfully within a few months she found a new cause to consume her energies. Anarchists and other groups in Spain were fighting a violent revolution against the Spanish monarchy. One of the leaders of the rebellion, Augustine Souchy, asked Goldman to become involved with this cause.

Goldman did not agree with the violent nature of the rebellion, and she thought the anarchists were betraying their ideals by forming a coalition with the communists in the conflict, but she had high hopes that a success for the forces of the Left could show the world an alternative to the Bolshevik regime in Russia. Ac-

Liberty Was Her Theme

Harry Weinberger, Emma's lawyer and friend for more than thirty years, presented one of the eulogies at Goldman's burial. Biographer Candace Falk includes a portion of that eulogy in Love, Anarchy, and Emma Goldman:

"Liberty was always her theme; liberty was always her dream; liberty was always her goal. . . . Emma Goldman in her lifetime had been ostracized, jailed, mobbed and deported from these shores for advocating that which all the world now admits should be brought about—a world without war, a world without poverty, a world with hope and the brotherhood of man. . . .

Emma Goldman, we welcome you back to America, where you wanted to end your days with friends and comrades. We had hoped to welcome you back in life—but we welcome you back in death. You will live forever in the hearts of your friends and the story of your life will live as long as stories are told of women and men of courage and idealism."

Mourners pay their respects as Goldman's casket is carried to a burial site in Chicago, Illinois. Goldman would be eulogized as a courageous activist for individual rights.

cordingly, she traveled to England and later to Canada, where she lived for a time, raising public support and funds for the revolution. She continued this effort into 1940, writing a pamphlet, "The Place of the Individual in Society," that addressed once more the familiar themes of the "beautiful idea" of an anarchist utopia:

> The interests of the State and those of the individual differ fundamentally and are antagonistic. The State and the political and economic institutions it supports can exist only by fashioning the individual to their particular purpose; training him to respect "law and order"; teaching him obedience, submission and unquestioning faith in the wisdom and justice of government. . . . The State puts itself and its interests even above the claims of religion and of God. . . . Of all social theories Anarchism alone steadfastly proclaims that society exists for man, not man for society. The sole legitimate purpose of society is to serve the needs and advance the aspiration of the individual.

> Only by doing so can it justify its existence and be an aid to progress and culture. . . . Man's quest for freedom from shackle is eternal. It must and will go on.[120]

The message remained substantially unchanged from those early days in New York City: honesty, beauty, individual freedom, and the liberty to pursue the ideals of happiness. Whatever impeded these pursuits was bad for the human condition, Goldman believed. Government, she was convinced, was everywhere and always repressive, unavoidably an obstacle to those goals. She committed herself to a fight against dominating governments to the end.

Emma Goldman was traveling in Canada on February 17, 1940, seeking funds for the revolution in Spain, when the end came. Paralyzed and silenced by a massive stroke, she never recovered, and she died May 14. Her body was returned to her "philosophical" home, Chicago, Illinois. There she was buried near the bodies of the Haymarket martyrs.

A Life Worth Living

In 1934 Emma Goldman wrote an essay that attempted to analyze her place in the struggle to obtain liberty for the individual. In this work, titled "Was My Life Worth Living?" she came to this positive conclusion:

> The fact that the Anarchist movement for which I have striven so long is to a certain extent in abeyance and overshadowed by philosophies of authority and coercion affects me with concern, but not despair. It seems to me a point of special significance that many countries decline to admit Anarchists. All governments hold the view that while parties of the right and left may advocate social changes, still they cling to the idea of government and authority. Anarchism alone breaks with both and propagates uncompromising rebellion. In the long run, therefore, it is Anarchism which is considered deadlier to the present regime than all other social theories that are now clamoring for power.

Considered from this angle, I think my life and my work have been successful. What is generally regarded as success—acquisition of wealth, the capture of power or social prestige—I consider the most dismal failures. I

Goldman continued her fight against oppressive governments until the end of her life, striving "to remain in a state of flux and continued growth, and not to petrify in a niche of self-satisfaction."

hold when it is said of a man that he has arrived, it means that he is finished—his development has stopped at that point. I have always striven to remain in a state of flux and continued growth, and not to petrify in a niche of self-satisfaction. If I had my life to live over again, like everyone else, I should wish to alter minor details. But in any of my more important actions and attitudes I would repeat my life as I have lived it. Certainly I should work for Anarchism with the same devotion and confidence in its ultimate triumph.[121]

Advancing the Cause of Freedom

During her lifetime Emma Goldman helped advance the cause of freedom of expression for herself and many others. Then, forgotten for nearly three decades after her death, some of the views Goldman expressed were again brought to life during the late 1960s and early 1970s with the antiwar and feminist movements in the United States. Goldman became a model for characters in novels, plays, and movies, partly because of her flamboyant and dramatic lifestyle but primarily because of her courage to challenge the accepted beliefs, customs, and intellectual and political convictions of the time. Many of her articles, books, and pamphlets have been republished and have inspired numerous activists in recent times to protest government and authoritarian interference in their lives.

Emma Goldman acted on the belief that an individual can make a difference in the social structure. Her organization of branches of the Free Speech League laid the foundation for the American Civil Liberties Union, established to protect such individual civil rights as the right to a fair trial, the right of free speech, and the right to vote. In the end, Emma Goldman's life and work underscored her view that people the world over love freedom and that, however authority may try to stamp it out, "freedom is the soul of progress and essential to every phase of life."[122]

Notes

Chapter 1: Foundations of a Revolutionary

1. Alix Shulman, *To the Barricades: The Anarchist Life of Emma Goldman*. New York: Thomas Y. Crowell, 1971.

2. Shulman, *To the Barricades*.

3. Emma Goldman, *Living My Life*, 2 vols. 1931. Reprinted New York: Knopf, 1970.

4. Goldman, *Living My Life*.

5. Goldman, *Living My Life*.

6. Goldman, *Living My Life*.

7. Goldman, *Living My Life*.

8. Goldman, *Living My Life*.

9. Goldman, *Living My Life*.

10. Goldman, *Living My Life*.

11. Goldman, *Living My Life*.

12. Quoted in Goldman, *Living My Life*.

13. Hippolyte Havel, "Emma Goldman," in Emma Goldman, *Anarchism and Other Essays*. 1910. Reprinted New York: Dover, 1969.

14. Goldman, *Living My Life*.

Chapter 2: Coming of Age in America

15. Goldman, *Living My Life*.

16. Goldman, *Living My Life*.

17. Quoted in Goldman, *Living My Life*.

18. Goldman, *Living My Life*.

19. Quoted in Goldman, *Living My Life*.

20. Goldman, *Living My Life*.

21. Quoted in Alan Dawley, "The International Working People's Association," in Dave Roediger and Franklin Rosemont, eds., *Haymarket Scrapbook*. Chicago: Charles H. Kerr, 1986.

22. Robert Hunter, *Violence and the Labor Movement*. 1914. Reprinted New York: Arno Press & The New York Times, 1969.

23. Quoted in Roediger and Rosemont, *Haymarket Scrapbook*.

24. Quoted in Candace Serena Falk, *Love, Anarchy, and Emma Goldman*. New Brunswick, NJ: Rutgers University Press, 1990.

25. Goldman, *Living My Life*.

26. Goldman, *Anarchism and Other Essays*.

27. Goldman, *Living My Life*.

28. Goldman, *Living My Life*.

29. Goldman, *Living My Life*.

Chapter 3: Dedicated to "the Cause"

30. Goldman, *Living My Life*.

31. Goldman, *Living My Life*.

32. Goldman, *Living My Life*.

33. Quoted in Goldman, *Living My Life*.

34. Goldman, *Living My Life*.

35. Goldman, *Living My Life*.

36. Goldman, *Living My Life*.

37. Goldman, *Living My Life*.

38. Goldman, *Living My Life*.

39. Goldman, *Living My Life*.

40. Goldman, *Living My Life*.

41. Quoted in Richard Drinnon, *Rebel in Paradise: A Biography of Emma Goldman*. Chicago: University of Chicago Press, 1961.

42. Hunter, *Violence and the Labor Movement*.

43. Quoted in Alice Wexler, *Emma Goldman: An Intimate Life*. New York: Pantheon, 1984.

44. Goldman, *Living My Life*.

45. Quoted in Drinnon, *Rebel in Paradise*.

46. Quoted in Goldman, *Living My Life*.

Chapter 4: "Red Emma"

47. Goldman, *Living My Life*.

48. Goldman, *Living My Life*.

49. Goldman, *Living My Life*.

50. Goldman, *Living My Life*.

51. Goldman, *Living My Life*.

52. Drinnon, *Rebel in Paradise*.

53. Goldman, *Living My Life*.

54. Quoted in Goldman, *Living My Life*.

55. Quoted in Drinnon, *Rebel in Paradise*.

56. Quoted in Wexler, *Emma Goldman*.

57. Goldman, *Living My Life*.

58. Goldman, *Living My Life*.

59. Goldman, *Living My Life*.

60. Goldman, *Living My Life*.

61. Goldman, *Living My Life*.

62. Goldman, *Living My Life*.

63. Quoted in Drinnon, *Rebel in Paradise*.

64. Wexler, *Emma Goldman*.

65. Quoted in Alix Kates Shulman, ed., *Red Emma Speaks: Selected Writings and Speeches by Emma Goldman*. New York: Random House, 1972.

Chapter 5: The Assassination of President McKinley

66. Goldman, *Living My Life*.

67. Goldman, *Living My Life*.

68. Goldman, *Living My Life*.

69. Goldman, *Living My Life*.

70. Wexler, *Emma Goldman*.

71. Goldman, *Living My Life*.

72. Quoted in Goldman, *Living My Life*.

73. Quoted in Wexler, *Emma Goldman*.

74. Quoted in Drinnon, *Rebel in Paradise*.

75. Quoted in Drinnon, *Rebel in Paradise*.

76. Goldman, *Living My Life*.

Chapter 6: From "Red Emma" to Mother Earth

77. Goldman, *Living My Life*.

78. Goldman, *Living My Life*.

79. Goldman, *Living My Life*.

80. Goldman, *Living My Life*.

81. Goldman, *Living My Life*.

82. Quoted in Drinnon, *Rebel in Paradise*.

83. Goldman, *Living My Life*.

84. Goldman, *Living My Life*.

85. Goldman, *Living My Life*.

86. Goldman, *Living My Life*.

87. Goldman, *Anarchism and Other Essays*.

88. Goldman, *Living My Life*.

Chapter 7: Government Victories

89. Quoted in Drinnon, *Rebel in Paradise*.

90. Shulman, *Red Emma Speaks*.

91. Quoted in Drinnon, *Rebel in Paradise*.

92. Goldman, *Living My Life*.

93. Goldman, *Living My Life*.

94. Goldman, *Living My Life*.

95. Quoted in Wexler, *Emma Goldman*.

96. Quoted in Shulman, *Red Emma Speaks*.

97. Quoted in Shulman, *Red Emma Speaks*.

98. Goldman, *Living My Life*.

99. Goldman, *Living My Life*.

100. Goldman, *Living My Life*.

101. Quoted in Drinnon, *Rebel in Paradise*.

102. Quoted in Drinnon, *Rebel in Paradise*.

Chapter 8: Life in Exile

103. Quoted in Wexler, *Emma Goldman*.

104. Goldman, *Living My Life*.

105. Goldman, *Living My Life*.

106. Goldman, *Living My Life.*
107. Goldman, *Living My Life.*
108. Goldman, *Living My Life.*
109. Goldman, *Living My Life.*
110. Quoted in Shulman, *Red Emma Speaks.*
111. Goldman, *Living My Life.*
112. Goldman, *Living My Life.*
113. Goldman, *Living My Life.*
114. Goldman, *Living My Life.*

Chapter 9: Endings

115. Quoted in Shulman, *Red Emma Speaks.*
116. Quoted in Falk, *Love, Anarchy, and Emma Goldman.*

117. Quoted in Falk, *Love, Anarchy, and Emma Goldman.*
118. Quoted in Martha Solomon, *Emma Goldman.* Boston: Twayne, 1987.
119. Quoted in Falk, *Love, Anarchy, and Emma Goldman.*
120. Quoted in Shulman, *Red Emma Speaks.*

Epilogue: A Life Worth Living

121. Quoted in Shulman, *Red Emma Speaks.*
122. Quoted in Shulman, *Red Emma Speaks.*

For Further Reading

John Chalberg, *Emma Goldman: American Individualist.* New York: HarperCollins, 1991. A young adult biography that traces Goldman's life from her birth in Russia through her immigration and life in the United States to her deportation and years of exile.

Richard Drinnon, *Rebel in Paradise: A Biography of Emma Goldman.* Chicago: University of Chicago Press, 1961. A critical biography of Emma Goldman brings alive the person who Drinnon says "provoked either warm support or furious opposition," with abundant evidence that "to the final breath [Goldman] waged an unrelenting fight for the free individual."

Barbara Alpern Engel and Clifford N. Rosenthal, eds. and trans., *Five Sisters: Women Against the Tsar.* New York: Knopf, 1975. Dedicated to "women fighting for freedom throughout the world," this compilation of memoirs of five Russian revolutionaries of the nineteenth century includes the story of Vera Zasulich, one of Emma Goldman's early heroines.

Candace Falk, *The Life and Times of Emma Goldman: A Curriculum for Middle and High School Students.* Berkeley: University of California Press, 1992. Primary historical documents on immigration, freedom of expression, women's rights, antimilitarism, and the art and literature of social change are presented for critical thinking and analysis in the context of Emma Goldman's life.

Andrea Hinding, ed., *Feminism.* San Diego: Greenhaven, 1986. Emma Goldman's views are included in debates that argue the pros and cons of marriage, women's suffrage, and the effect of feminism on contemporary society.

Alix Shulman, *To the Barricades: The Anarchist Life of Emma Goldman.* New York: Thomas Y. Crowell, 1971. A highly readable young adult book that includes black-and-white photographs and covers the major events in Goldman's life.

K. C. Tessendorf, *Kill the Tsar! Youth and Terrorism in Old Russia.* New York: Atheneum, 1986. An illustrated young adult book that covers the reign of Czar Alexander II of Russia and the radicals among his subjects who sought political reforms. Includes a dramatic chapter detailing the assassination of Alexander.

David Waldstreicher and Matina S. Horner, *Emma Goldman.* New York: Chelsea House, 1990. This biography of Emma Goldman is one in a series on American women of achievement. It follows the life of this Russian-born woman from the time she left Russia through her years in the United States as a champion of the oppressed and her life in exile.

Works Consulted

Candace Falk and Ronald R. Zboray, eds., *A Guide to the Emma Goldman Papers.* Alexandria, VA: 1991. A detailed guide to the more than forty thousand documents and approximately seventy reels of microfilm in the collection of The Emma Goldman Papers project at the University of California, Berkeley. The project was established in 1980 to organize, edit, and publish on microfilm letters and articles by and about Emma Goldman and government documents, newspaper clippings, photographs, and other materials on her life from twelve hundred sources worldwide.

Candace Serena Falk, *Love, Anarchy, and Emma Goldman.* New Brunswick, NJ: Rutgers University Press, 1990. A biography by the director of The Emma Goldman Papers project focuses on Goldman's love life and includes many excerpts from letters that show how her life was organized around issues of love and anarchy.

Emma Goldman, *Anarchism and Other Essays.* 1910. Reprinted with introduction, preface, and foreword by Hippolyte Havel. New York: Dover, 1969. First published in 1910, Goldman's collection of essays presents her views not only on anarchism but also on such topics as "The Psychology of Political Violence," "Prisons: A Social Crime and Failure," "Woman Suffrage," and "Marriage and Love."

Emma Goldman, *Living My Life*, 2 vols. 1931. Reprinted New York: Knopf, 1970. Goldman's frank and vivid autobiography begins with her twentieth year and continues through her deportation to Russia in 1919 and her exile in Europe, to her years of activism in England and Canada. But throughout the two volumes, Goldman recalls many events of her brutal early childhood in Russia, her immigration to the United States at age sixteen, and her first difficult years in the United States. Though events are not told in a strict chronological order, Goldman's life story unfolds in a seemingly effortless fashion.

Robert Hoffman, ed., *Anarchism.* New York: Atherton Press, 1970. Essays on anarchism by Emma Goldman and Alexander Berkman are included in this compilation of anarchist theories and criticism.

Robert Hunter, *Violence and the Labor Movement.* 1914. Reprinted New York: Arno Press & The New York Times, 1969. Writing not long after the assassination of President William McKinley and numerous violent labor strikes across the country, the author discusses the theories and deeds of European anarchists of the 1800s. Includes chapters on "Johann Most in America," "The Birth of Modern Socialism," rifts between socialists and anarchists, and anarchist activities in the United States.

Margaret S. Marsh, *Anarchist Women 1870–1920*. Philadelphia: Temple University Press, 1981. Women besides Emma Goldman became active members of the anarchist movement in the United States during Goldman's lifetime. They worked not only to restructure society but also because they wanted to go beyond women's traditional roles "in order to create for themselves independent, productive, and meaningful lives," according to the author. The book includes profiles of such anarchists as Goldman, Helena Born, and Voltairine de Cleyre, and other women activists working for voting rights, women's rights, and labor reform.

Marian Morton, *Emma Goldman and the American Left: "Nowhere at Home."* New York: Twayne, 1992. Although Emma Goldman stated that she never felt at home with any political movement, this book, part of the *Twentieth Century American Biography* series, shows the similarities between her particular form of anarchism and the radicalism prevalent in the United States during the late 1800s and early 1900s.

Richard O'Connor, *The German-Americans: An Informal History*. Boston: Little,

Brown, 1968. A chapter, "The Image Darkens," of this historical account of German immigrants in the United States briefly describes the philosophy of Chicago anarchists, the Haymarket riot, and the roles of Johann Most, Emma Goldman, and Alexander Berkman in the American anarchist movement.

Dave Roediger and Franklin Rosemont, eds., *Haymarket Scrapbook*. Chicago: Charles H. Kerr, 1986. A collection of articles, posters, songs, poems, and excerpts from letters covering the "Haymarket affair."

Alix Kates Shulman, ed., *Red Emma Speaks: Selected Writings and Speeches by Emma Goldman*. New York: Random House, 1972. Writings and speeches in this collection span nearly three decades, beginning with "What I Believe," in which Goldman explains her views on property, government, militarism, free speech, religion, marriage and love, and acts of violence. Sections include lectures first published in *Mother Earth* and articles published in other magazines and newspapers.

Martha Solomon, *Emma Goldman*. Boston: Twayne, 1987. Part of *United States Authors* series, this biography focuses on Goldman's life as reflected in articles, letters, and other writings.

Alice Wexler, *Emma Goldman: An Intimate Life*. New York: Pantheon, 1984. As the title indicates, this biography presents the private Goldman, revealing through personal letters her passions, moods, and fantasies. The biography also focuses on Goldman's commitment to feminism and the need to address women's issues during her time.

Alice Wexler, *Emma Goldman in Exile: From the Russian Revolution to the Spanish Civil War*. Boston: Beacon Press, 1989. A companion to her 1984 Goldman biography, this volume picks up Goldman's life following her deportation to Russia. Historian Wexler argues that Goldman, because of personal disappointments and disillusionment that anarchist ideals had not been realized in Russia, greatly exaggerated postrevolutionary terrorism there, which contributed to the long-held U.S. stereotype of communism as monstrous evil. The book covers her relationship with Alexander Berkman during the last years of his life, Goldman's activities during the Spanish Civil War, and her death at seventy.

Index

Picture Credits

Cover photo: Culver Pictures, Inc.

AP/Wide World Photos, 109, 110

The Bettmann Archive, 37, 72, 94 (both)

Brown Brothers, 42, 73, 90

Culver Pictures, Inc., 30 (top), 33, 44, 47, 52, 62, 64, 67, 84 (top), 92

David King Collection, 21, 69, 95, 97

International Institute of Social History, Amsterdam, 25, 35, 49, 51, 59, 66, 71, 76, 88, 99, 100, 106

Library of Congress, 9, 23, 24, 29, 39, 54, 56, 61, 78, 91, 103

National Archives, 85

North Wind Picture Archives, 12, 13, 18, 20, 70

Sophia Smith Collection, Smith College, 84 (bottom)

Special Collections Library, University of Michigan, 14, 16, 34

Stock Montage, Inc., 26, 30 (bottom), 50, 74, 101

UPI/Bettmann, 10, 79, 81, 86, 102, 105

About the Authors

Kathlyn Gay is the author of more than seventy books on diverse topics ranging from environmental and social issues to American history, folklore, and communication. Prior to *Emma Goldman*, she collaborated with her son Martin (Marty) Gay on a book about the Information Superhighway, a series of books about America's wars, an encyclopedia of North American eating and drinking rituals, customs, and traditions, and two books on vegetarianism. Ms. Gay and her husband, Arthur Gay, a retired teacher and school administrator, live in Elkhart, Indiana. Their two other children, Douglas and Karen, live in the Midwest and have also collaborated on book projects.

Martin Gay lives in Port Townsend, Washington, with his wife, Michelle, and son, Dakota. His daughter, Nissa, lives in Southern California. Marty's eclectic background includes a degree in economics from the University of Notre Dame, work as a classroom teacher, educational consultant, television producer and director, chef, restaurateur, Internet trainer, and writer. He is currently director of ELTEC, a visionary pilot project to connect learning and community using the Internet in five Washington state school districts. He is also nurturing a new "Virtual Faculty" of Internet trainers who are volunteering to teach teachers the tools of digital information retrieval.